THE RV
LIFESTYLE
MANUAL

Living as a Boondocking Expert
How to Swap Your Day Job for Travel
and Adventure on the Open Road

JEREMY FROST

© Copyright 2019 Jeremy Frost - All rights reserved.

It is not legal to reproduce, duplicate, or transmit any part of this document in either electronic means or in printed format. Recording of this publication is strictly prohibited, and any storage of this document is not allowed unless with written permission from the publisher except for the use of brief quotations in a book review.

ISBN: 9781701917224 (Paperback)

CONTENTS

Introduction 1

Chapter 1: You Have Way Too Much Stuff! 7

    Downsizing for the Count 9

    Evaluating Future Purchases 25

Chapter 2: Choosing the Right RV for You 27

    Points to Remember Before Buying an RV 27

    Important Myths to Debunk 37

    Types of RVs 40

    Floor Plans to Think About 46

    Learning to Drive Your RV 51

Chapter 3: Transitioning into the RV Lifestyle 57

    Adjusting to Your New Life on the Road 58

    How to Survive Living in a Small Space! 60

    Traveling With Kids and Animals 66

    Tips for RVing With Pets 72

    Making Your RV Feel like Home 75

Chapter 4: What You Need to Know Before You Go! 81

- How Do You Dump the Tanks? 81
- Regular Maintenance on the Road 88
- Why Your RV Needs to be Level 92
- What to Do If the RV Breaks Down 96
- Electricity and Power 100

Chapter 5: Camping and Boondocking Basics 109

- What is Boondocking All About? 109
- How to Camp for Free All Over the World 110
- RV Clubs and Memberships 118
- Long-Term and Short-Term Parking Options for Your RV .. 121

Chapter 6: Making Money on the Road 125

- Finding Seasonal Work 126
- Why Freelance Work Might Be Right for You 129
- Working at the Campground 132
- How to Start Earning Passive Income Online 133

Chapter 7: Solo RVing Done Right 143

- Don't Let Being by Yourself Stop You! 144
- Staying Safe on the Road 148
- Avoiding Loneliness 150

Connecting With the Community 156

Chapter 8: Commonly Asked Questions 161

What is the worst thing about living in an RV? 161

What is the best thing about RV life? 162

How can you do laundry? 164

Do you feel safe on the road? 165

Isn't gas mileage terrible? 166

When will you start living a normal life again? 167

Can you RV full-time in the winter? 167

How do you stay in shape while on the road? 168

Do you get tired of living in a small space? 168

What do you do with all the poop? 168

Conclusion 169

References 171

Life is either a daring adventure or nothing at all.
– *Helen Keller*

INTRODUCTION

Imagine visiting a peaceful town one day, eating the local cuisine and checking out the sights, and then traveling past scenic views and gorgeous vistas the next.

A lot of people might say, "Aren't you talking about a backpacker lifestyle?"

Hardly. I am talking about the RV lifestyle.

If the backpacker lifestyle is like Tony Stark before he created the Iron Man suit, then the RV lifestyle is like Tony with the nanosuit he used in the final *Avengers* movie; you are surrounded by awesome tech, you have abundant comfort and amenities, and you can travel better than a backpacker.

If you haven't watched *The Avengers* or any of the Marvel movies and failed to get the above reference, then let's try looking at it this way:

Would you enjoy walking with a backpack strapped to your body as you hitchhike your way around the country, trying to replenish your cash reserves while thinking of where you might find a decent place to sleep? Or would you prefer to move around in a comfortable land vehicle that looks like a studio apartment on wheels?

The RV lifestyle is the answer to the nine-to-five grind. It is the wake-up call that you have been waiting for, letting you know that if you are indeed planning on spending most of your time in an enclosed space (a.k.a. your office), then you might as well do it in one that keeps moving from one place to another (a.k.a. in an RV). You are meant to experience the world, but that might not happen if you take the elevator (or, for the unlucky ones, the stairs) to the same place every single day. And if you are among those wondering how you are going to break free from this monotonous lifestyle, an RV is your answer.

Of course, after answering the 'what,' where you figured out what you are supposed to do to change the course of your life, you are then stuck with another important question.

How?

How are you going to get into an RV and move around without enough resources? How are you going to procure food, fuel, and other basic necessities? How can you continue to earn a stable income while you are on the road?

All your answers are going to be provided by this book. You are going to learn about the fundamentals behind downsizing from a house or a condo to an RV. Once you reduce the space you are living in to the interior of your mobile home, then you are going to learn how to travel full-time (never thought you would hear the words, "travel full-time," did you?).

We are even going to examine what kind of RV you should purchase. This is to ensure you are not looking at an RV and probably thinking of getting a loan, selling everything you have, and making a deal with the devil just to get it. You are going to be guided through what supplies you might need to pack into the RV and where you could stay while you are traveling. This book is not just aiming to be informative; it is aiming to be the instruction manual to your RV lifestyle.

But why me? Of all the people in the world, what makes me an RV expert?

It is because I have lived the RV lifestyle. Actually, let me rephrase that. I have been a part of the RV lifestyle since I was young.

My parents were avid campers. They loved the outdoors and living life with the simple joy of experiencing what this world can offer us. Imagine this: you are surrounded by the stillness of nature, or the sounds of nature's inhabitants. There is the unmistakable smell of freshness that you cannot easily find in a city. All around you are spectacular views that you thought you would never see in your lifetime.

Whenever it was time to go RVing, my parents and I wouldn't just spend a few hours or a few days outside; we would be out there for several months! And that's how I grew familiar with the lifestyle, understanding all there is to know about how to live in an RV, what to do when you are moving around, and how to become part of the lifestyle. In fact, my dad used to use his RV to drive me to my daily baseball games. A single activity that used to only take place over several months eventually became a significant part of my life.

Fast forward to the present. I have now spent over five years traveling around the world in motorhomes, campers, and vans. I know one thing about this life, and that is that it is quite fleeting. I had to ask myself if it was worth spending my days simply dredging through the mundanity of life, or if I could do something more to live better. With that being said, I hope this book gives you the motivation to get into your RV and hit the road, if you haven't already done so.

Once you have read this book, you are going to have the tools to become part of an adventure. You are going to discover how you can embrace freedom and travel, without being attached to the corporate rat race.

Think about it.

You now have no schedule. There is no compulsion to attend a meeting and explain your tasks for the day, or the targets you had missed by a minute margin. You won't have to indulge in office politics just so you can have a better standing with the boss man or woman. There is no need to be competitive with anyone.

Your life is in your hands, and you are going to drive it (both literally and metaphorically).

And guess what? You are not the first person who I have helped embrace this lifestyle. I've worked with hundreds of people who are in the same position you are in right now. They knew that they wanted to take destiny by the reins (or in this case, the steering wheel), and make a difference in their lives. I have helped them make that difference.

And now, it is your turn.

You don't have to be an expert on RVs or camping. All you need to do is have that mindset of wanting to make a difference in your life. When you have confirmed that you indeed do want to make this change, then don't think about making it 'someday.' The truth about the 'someday' statement is that, usually, those things don't happen, or if they do, they occur in a manner you might not be satisfied with.

So get ready to enter a journey, as each chapter in this book will take you that much closer to your goal.

Get ready to swap your day job for travel and adventure on the open road.

Let's rev this journey!

CHAPTER 1
You Have Way Too Much Stuff!

You might have a lot of possessions with you right now. Just look around and you'll find a visual confirmation of that statement.

When you are about to make the shift to living full-time in an RV, you are going to have to make some important decisions. Mostly, you are going to make the not-so-easy choice of figuring out just what you would like to have in your RV. If you quickly assess all the things you have in your home, you are likely going to feel that there are many things that are important to you. But importance does not mean you can take them with you—you can't fit your entire shoe wardrobe into your RV. You are going to have to make some choices.

At this point, you might be thinking about how difficult it is going to be, parting with some of your possessions. You might even wonder if there are others out there who are about to go through the same dilemma you are going to face. Isn't the world heading towards the ownership of more materialistic things, rather than walking away from them?

Do you want to know the reality of the situation? People are actually giving up on materialistic possessions in exchange for experiences. In fact, it has been estimated that over 78% of millennials—who have an astonishing $1.3 trillion purchasing power—are choosing to spend that hard-earned money on experiences rather than objects (Power, 2018).

The point is that more and more people are less afraid to give up on things in exchange for something more valuable: the chance to live through something intangible and wonderful. However, the problem they face is not knowing how to keep on living the life they choose. They find themselves saving up some money, traveling to a country and experiencing new things, then returning back to their day jobs. Rinse and repeat. They are not able to keep the traveling lifestyle sustainable.

Nevertheless, what we are going to do is not merely travel someplace and return back to our daily grind. We are going to keep on traveling for as long as our hearts desire.

With that idea in mind, it becomes less difficult to get rid of some of the things currently taking up space in your home.

DOWNSIZING FOR THE COUNT

Let's get down to the nitty-gritty details of the downsizing process. Remember that it does not matter if you are living in a beachfront property or a small studio. Downsizing is a tough job, unless you have been living a minimalist lifestyle, in which case, you might find the task of preparing your RV considerably easier.

To clearly explain the concept of downsizing, I have broken down the process into simple steps.

A Downsizing Plan

Your plan brings together various factors to help keep the downsizing process running smoothly. To develop an effective downsizing plan, think of the below points or questions while keeping in mind the space in the RV you are moving into (which we will discuss in the next chapter):

- What items from your home can you get rid of?
- What can you absolutely not get rid of?

- How can you donate, sell, or throw away items that you won't need?
- Which items will you donate, sell, or throw away?

Items You Cannot Get Rid Of

This is a difficult junction in the downsizing process, mostly because of the fact that if we ask ourselves what we would like to get rid of, we might just answer by saying, "Absolutely nothing!"

But in order to find out what you should keep, think of the following points or questions:

- Are there any items that have sentimental value to you?
- Think of those items that you have spent a lot of money on and loathe to part with it.
- Write a list of the items you have held onto for a long time.
- Do you have objects or items you haven't used yet, but think they hold potential for the future?

Once you have made a list of the items you cannot get rid of, try giving a reason as to why you cannot let go of them.

This is an important step because, oftentimes, we are unsure of the actual reason why we would like to hold on to some things. That pocket watch your father gave you when you were young is something you should always hold on to. But the $300 shoes you bought thinking they would impress your friends won't really matter for your RV life. When you start evaluating your arsenal of items with logic and rational thought, then you can actually begin to understand what you should include in your RV and what you can get rid of.

Downsize Your Clothes

Now that you have a pile of clothes you cannot get rid of, look through those items again and pick the pieces you will need while you are RVing. In order to make it a little bit easier on you, here is a list of necessary items:

- Casual t-shirts and shorts
- A few button-up shirts
- A couple formal wear (or dress) options
- Jeans
- Slacks and track shirts/pants (if you have them)
- Windbreaker and fleece jacket
- Raincoat

- A pair of casual shoes and a pair of formal shoes/shoes that go with formal wear (essentially, nothing that looks appropriate for jogging)
- Hiking boots, or boots for cold weather
- Bathrobe
- Night clothes
- Slippers
- Sandals
- Bathroom slippers
- Sunglasses
- Wraparound glasses with wind protection
- A few face masks (for those who have certain allergies or for any other reason that might come up)
- Umbrellas (one should be enough, but you could keep a couple if you have space)

Donate or Sell Your Clothes

While you are downsizing your wardrobe, think about the items that you could donate to a local charity or other non-profit organizations. At this point, you might feel like you have many clothes you would not like to part with, but the key is to think of downsizing in a logical manner. For example, if you have a dozen dresses, pick one or two you really like and keep the rest for donation or sale. It's the same with everything else. If you have a shoe closet with about 200 different pairs of shoes, you won't be needing all of them on your trip. Make a rational decision and let the rest go to someone in need.

Trash Your Clothes

If you have clothes that are faded, have stains or tears, or might be damaged beyond repair, throw them away. Some people might decide to donate such clothes, but I like to believe that if you don't like wearing them, don't give them to someone else. If you are giving something away, make sure it is in relatively good condition. It's a matter of principle similar to the idea that if you wouldn't eat something, don't give the food to someone else.

Store Some Clothes

You might come across certain clothes that have a sentimental value. Don't bring them in your RV. Rather, store them in your home for safekeeping. If there are any other items of clothing you simply must store, then make sure you do it now.

Essential Kitchen Items to Take

You know what they say—if you don't prepare, then you'd better beware.

Actually, nobody said that, but you can't deny that it is true. When you plan ahead, then you are not leaving anything to chance. You're making the right moves and choices to ensure that you have greater control over as many future scenarios as possible. While it is true that the future is uncertain and we cannot always prepare for every outcome, it goes without saying that you should expect the best and prepare for the worst. And yes, somebody actually said that.

Your next course of action is to take all the items you will require in your mobile kitchen. Here is a handy list you can use as a template:

- Dinner plates, coffee mugs, cereal bowls, dessert dishes
- Drinking and wine glasses
- Chef's knife
- Spoons (both tablespoons and teaspoons), forks, and dinner knives
- Whisk
- Grater
- Cutting board

- Can opener
- Measuring cups and measuring spoons
- Colander
- Mixing bowls
- Vegetable peeler
- Potato masher
- Tongs
- Corkscrew or wine bottle opener
- Stainless steel skillet
- Saucepans (one small, one medium, and one large)
- Baking sheet pan
- Casserole dish
- Cookie sheet
- Storage containers
- Aluminum foil
- Plastic wrap
- Oven mittens
- Immersion blender
- Plastic tablecloth
- Table mats, dish cloths, and napkins
- Clips to close bags
- Heavy sponge
- Dishwashing liquid
- Small trash bags

- Coffee pot (get a percolator one on the off chance you don't have a sufficient power source)
- Small grill
- BBQ utensils
- Small toaster

Kitchen Items to Donate or Sell

Here are points to consider when you are donating or selling kitchen items:

- Items that are duplicates.
- Things that you might not need for an RV, like cheese spreaders, salad spinners, and garlic presses.
- Other items you do not use often.

Kitchen Items to Trash

Just like your clothing, throw away any kitchen item that is broken, damaged, or rusted.

Essential Bedding/Sofa Items to Take

Time to add a bit of comfort in your RV. For the most part, choosing the items you would like to take for bedding (or sofa, if your RV has one) is fairly simple. Nevertheless, here is a handy list for inspiration:

- Pillows and a few pillowcases
- At least one change of bed linens
- Comforter
- Blankets
- A few cushions
- Your favorite soft toy, if you have one (hey, no judgment passed—it's your RV!)

Bedding Items to Donate or Sell

- Items that are too bulky or are not required for an RV, such as large cushions, bed linens that are too big, curtains, and anything of the like.
- Any duplicates, ranging from your pillowcases to bedspreads.

Bedding Items to Store

If you have certain items with sentimental value, keep them with you. Plan everything carefully so you don't accidentally give away or sell something that might later prove to be valuable to you or to someone else.

Documents to Keep in the RV

There are those documents you would like to always have with you, just in case a situation occurs where you might need to show them as proof of something or to complete a process. Below is a list that should help you get started, but feel free to add anything you think is absolutely invaluable.

- Passports, birth certificates, marriage documents, and documents that prove the purchase of the RV.
- Multiple copies of all the above documents.
- Any insurance you may need.
- Multiple copies of all the above documents.
- Multiple passport-size photographs.
- Identification cards, credit cards, insurance cards (if you have them), social security cards (if you have them), and other forms or cards or special identifications. Also, make sure you have multiple copies of these documents as well.
- If you have important records, such as tax records, consider scanning them all and storing them electronically. Since records might be useful, however, you can keep them with you in the RV as well.

Documents to Donate or Sell

I'm just kidding. I would never ask you to donate or sell any documents! And for that matter, let's assume you are not supposed to send any documents to the trash. However, we do need to add one additional section here that is going to be quite useful.

Documents to Store Electronically

It is going to be difficult getting rid of those framed photographs of your family, but rather than put all of them together into boxes, simply upload them into a cloud space or an online storage platform.

Additionally, make sure that as many documents as possible under the "Documents to Keep in the RV" section are stored electronically, both to save on space and make them easier to locate if and when you need them.

Office Supplies to Keep in Your RV

Make sure you bring your laptop or computer and all the cables and devices that go along with it. One of the most efficient ways to store all these cables is by putting them in Ziplock bags, where each bag is used for one cable. If you need an additional cable for certain types (such as an HDMI), then you can put both in the same Ziplock.

If you have space, bring your printer or scanner as well, but it is not necessary to do so. When short on space, store any other additional electronic devices in your home.

Keep a ream of A4-sized paper with you, along with a couple of the below items (except in the case of paper clips and safety pins, where you can keep a small box of them):

- Pens and pencils
- Erasers
- Pencil sharpeners
- Notepads
- Tape
- Permanent markers and highlighters (just choose one or two colors)
- Staplers
- Paper clips
- Safety pins

Office Items to Put into Storage

Do not take too many pens or office supplies with you. It might be nice to have 200 different kinds of pens, but you won't be needing all of them on your travels. Pare down to the necessities and store the rest away.

Tools for Your RV

On your journey, it might be useful to have a few tools with you to deal with any emergency situations. I have created a handy list for you below—but note that you don't have to have every single tool from the list. If space is a concern, at least make sure you bring the essential ones.

Essential Items

- Assorted tools such as hammers, wrenches, screwdrivers, and pliers
- Assorted nails, screws, and bolts
- One small bucket
- Drill and bits
- One extension cord (if you have space, add in another one)
- Water filter for the RV
- Flashlights
- Batteries
- Hoses (you can get different- colored ones, where one is used for regular water and the other for drinking water)
- Jumper cables

- Rubber gloves for cleaning and emptying tanks
- Soap and a brush for washing the vehicle
- Zip ties
- WD40

Non-essential Items

- Ax
- Bungee cords (might also become useful if you are into extreme sports)
- Work gloves and coveralls (not entirely necessary, but add it if you have them around in your home)
- Flare kit
- Measuring tape
- Brake transmission fluid, power steering fluid, and motor oil (you can also get these at a nearby gas station)
- Shovel

Tools You Should Store

Put all the stuff like paint, electronic tools, and other hardware, into storage. Make sure you are absolutely strict about storing such tools because a lot of them will require significant space if you try to bring them into your RV.

Additional Items

If you have the space for it, you can also add in a couple of outdoor folding chairs, a grill, a small folding table, and an outdoor mat.

You can also attach a step ladder to the back of the RV. This is useful when you need to do cleaning and maintenance activities on the top of your vehicle.

Take road maps, guides, and other useful navigational books and documents with you. Of course, you can always find everything you need on your phone—as long as you have an Internet connection.

The key phrase in the above statement is "as long as you have an Internet connection." Sometimes, you might need assistance when you have low connectivity or no service whatsoever.

Selling Your House After Moving Into an RV

Once again, I'm only joking. Please don't sell your house! There are a few ways you can earn income through your house while you travel, but more on that later. For now, let us look at just one more section.

Hobbies You Can Bring to Your RV

Obviously, you cannot pack all your possible hobbies into your RV. Some of them, like gardening, are things you just won't be able to do, especially with the equipment that is required. However, there are certain activities you can include in your RV (and maybe even adopt as a new hobby).

- If you are into painting, you can pack in an easel and some paints if you have the space for it.
- Books can be digitized, so you might want to subscribe to Amazon or Kobo books to get all your reading material.
- Stiching, crocheting, and wood carving can also be made portable.
- Pack a single guitar if you can, but otherwise most musical instruments won't fit into the RV. If you can find instruments that are the size of the guitar or smaller and you can find the extra space, bring them along.

EVALUATING FUTURE PURCHASES

In this section, make a list of the things you might purchase in the future. You will likely need to brainstorm a little bit, but making this list will help you greatly during your travels.

- You will tend to avoid any clutter in the future. When you plan ahead, you know the space you have in your RV and your purchases will be made accordingly.
- With proper planning, you can think long and hard about the things you want. Sometimes, you might feel like some items need to be added to your already growing pile of things, but upon careful evaluation, you might find alternatives.
- When you make a list of the things you would like to purchase, you might automatically start checking to see if you still have some of the essential items with you. If, as you go through the list, you notice your supply of staples is getting low, make a quick purchase (if you would like to replenish staples).
- Keep everything organized in its own space so that it is easy to check for inventory, which will also help you get an idea of what space you might have for future purchases.

- Whenever you add something to your purchase list, think of the dimensions and weight of the object you are adding. This will allow you to plan your RV space much more efficiently.

So, you see, with the right planning, you can make the most use of your space. But what's the point of all that downsizing if you don't even have an RV? After all, that is going to be your first decision: the choice of mobile home you would like to invest in.

For that reason, I shall let my esteemed and knowledgeable colleague, Sir Chapter 2, take over.

CHAPTER 2
Choosing the Right RV for You

Right now, I'm sure you are excited to jump into the details of the various types of RVs you can invest in. That's really good; you need to have that excitement. However, there are a few factors that you have to think about before you even consider buying an RV.

POINTS TO REMEMBER BEFORE BUYING AN RV

Buying an RV is not as simple as getting a new car (which is also not a simple decision). There are some essential criteria you need to think about. Some people think that considering the below points dashes their hopes of ever owning an RV, but I beg to differ. I think you have to be realistic when you are buying an RV. In fact, this point goes for any big investment you make throughout your life.

Think about it, how long did it take you to decide to buy your home or move into an apartment? You must have checked out the location, price, amenities, accessibility to transportation, internet access, building materials, age of the building, neighborhood, and probably a dozen other factors before you decided to buy, rent, or lease the place.

Let us look at some of the requirements you should consider before you decide to buy your RV.

Point #1: Type of Camping

Think about the type of camping that you would like to do. For the purpose of this book, we are going to assume that you will be in your RV full-time.

However, if you would like to focus on primitive camping, you could think about investing in a travel trailer or a pop-up tent.

For our purpose, however, we are going to be looking at Class As, Class Cs, airstreams, or maybe even vintages—but more on that later in this chapter.

Point #2: Your Journey

It is important to have a rough idea of the places you would like to travel to. By knowing this, you can understand what kind of RV you would like to get.

For example, if you are thinking of staying at public parks, then you should ideally consider getting an RV that is no more than 32 feet. With smaller units, you won't encounter many problems.

If you are thinking of investing in bigger RVs, then you should also think about the stops you are going to make on your journey. Where are some of the ideal places you can do with an RV of the size that you are going to get?

The important thing to remember about this point is that you don't have to get into the details of the journey; that's for another chapter. You are simply developing a rough idea to help you make an appropriate purchase decision.

Point #3: *Stay for Long or Travel Constantly?*

The bigger the RV, the more fuel it consumes. This could become an important factor in deciding what kind of RV you would like for longer travels. Furthermore, it is not just about the size, but all the features packed into the vehicle. More electrical components means more fuel for your journey.

On the flipside, if you are planning to stay in one spot for a longer duration, then you should think about what your vehicle can offer you in terms of everyday living requirements.

When you are traveling, you might also want to consider the terrain you may traverse. If you are planning to ride off the beaten track, consider the overall build of the RV. Most vehicles are built low to the ground, which means navigating through uneven terrain may pose as a challenge for your RV. Remember that RV maintenance may be expensive, so damaging it frequently is really going to put a dent in your wallet.

Point #4: RV Occupants

How many people are going to travel in the RV? Are you going to be bringing any pets? If so, will they need to go outside frequently, or are they just indoor pets? Are kids going to join you in the RV? Do you need a small space for them to play or study?

The above questions will help you choose an RV that offers sufficient space to provide for all your answers. For example, if you have a camper van, then you are not going to be able to fit two dogs and your family, as well.

Point #5: Your Budget

This is probably something you will be taking into account a lot. To be honest, not many people like thinking about the budget, but it is important to take note of your finances. More importantly, you need to have a realistic projection of your purchase. Let's say you are planning to spend just under $50,000 for an RV because that is all you will require. That's great! Perhaps you are going to be traveling alone and don't need all the extra baggage or people. But then again, after considering all the previous options, you may think of investing in a bigger RV, yet realize you can easily shell out $150,000 (key word here is 'easily') for a well-appointed vehicle. You should not be in a position where you are borrowing money from different sources for your RV. If you are, there is a separate section below for you that you need to take a look at. You might also need to consider the possibility of a fifth wheel and a truck, but more on that in Point #7.

Point #6: Getting Money

I don't recommend this option. The reason why you are shifting to a mobile home is not just to downsize in reality, but in your life as well. You are minimizing the influence of materialistic objects, living your life to the fullest, and avoiding the stress of bills and debts. If you start borrowing money from the bank or other financial institutions, then your debts will follow you wherever you go. No open space will eliminate the presence of impending loans from your mind.

For your peace of mind, try not to borrow money.

However, an RV is an expensive investment, so I can understand the need to consider financing options. For that reason, here are a few tips to consider:

- Make sure you calculate your loan amount and the monthly payment scheme. When you are calculating this, you need to make it as realistic as possible. Do not try and give yourself wiggle room. This is your future and finances we are talking about, after all.
- When calculating the debt payment scheme, make sure you include all the expenses you might require while using your RV. Do you have enough for the loans you have taken? Can you comfortably pay off what you've borrowed?
- Do not borrow any amount you cannot pay back within two years. I don't recommend working on your loan for more than two years because of the stress it could bring to your life. Think about this way, do you really want to spend more than the first couple of years of your RV life worrying about loans?

- Keep a strict budget during the payment period. Do not overspend when you are living in the RV. Make sure that you prioritize your basic needs first (including fuel for the RV and other such expenses), then focus on your debts, and finally on anything else that you require.
- I've said this before and I am going to repeat it again: expect the best and prepare for the worst. What happens during a medical emergency? What about urgent repairs to your RV? Are you able to pay for such expenses and still pay back your debts?
- Would you need to invest in a fifth wheel and a truck? If so, are you able to meet those investments and pay off your debts, as well?

As you can see, borrowing money is a pretty tough choice. Make sure you are absolutely certain of your decision. If you think your mind is rather biased towards the idea of a loan because you are tempted to get a fancy RV, then seek advice from your friends, family, or experts in your area. Get a second and third opinion before you think about borrowing any money.

Point #7: Truck

If you are planning to get yourself a travel trailer, then you might need a truck or a fifth wheel.

So, what exactly is this 'fifth wheel' we are talking about? It sounds like four wheels are going on a double date, and Mr. Fifth Wheel is all by himself.

That's not the kind of fifth wheel we are talking about, and quite frankly, I think the term 'third wheel' is used for anybody, regardless of how many people they are with.

But I digress; back to the point I am trying to make. A fifth wheel is a coupling mechanism that is used to attach the truck to the trailer.

The above point might be a little confusing, so let me break it down for you.

There are two types of travel trailers: those that are attached to the back bumper of a truck, or any other form of towing vehicle, and those attached to the bed of the towing vehicle. A ball-and-coupler hitch mechanism is typically used to attach the trailer to the towing vehicle. A fifth-wheel trailer, on the other hand, is not attached to your rear bumper. Rather, it is connected to the bed of a truck or the towing vehicle using a special jaw hitch. As you can see, if you are getting a travel trailer, then you should ideally have a truck that is big enough to pull it. If you are planning on getting a fifth-wheel trailer, you might need to invest in the fifth wheel mechanism.

Think about this when you are considering your RV choices.

Point #8: The Driver

This might sound like an odd point to make note of, but trust me when I say that it might be useful in the long run. If you have people traveling with you and would like to share the driving responsibilities with someone else, then you need to get an RV that is convenient for both you and the other person to drive.

If you need to check out how it feels like to be in the RV of your choosing, you can try taking one out for a test run. This will give you a sense of what you are buying, or if you would like to consider a different purchase.

Point #9: Features

You should ideally think about the features if you have sufficient funds to pay for them, as the more features an RV has, the more expensive it might get. Different RVs provide different features. The best way to choose something that is right for you is to consider your lifestyle. Think of some of the luxuries you used to enjoy and see if you can afford them when it comes to your RV.

Here are a few options you might think about:

- Television
- Bunk bed
- Dining table
- Washer and dryer
- Multipurpose areas
- A desk
- Basement storage
- Two bathrooms

Once you have considered the above, and all the other points in this list, then you are able to make an informed decision about your RV.

But while we are on the subject of important points to think about, it is time we dispel some myths that have cropped up around RVs and RV lifestyles.

IMPORTANT MYTHS TO DEBUNK

Myth #1: RVs are Cheap

While you can find inexpensive options and perhaps even get a second-hand vehicle at a highly discounted rate, there is no such thing as a cheap RV.

Once you purchase your RV, there are additional maintenance, upkeep, and repair costs you have to think about. At one point in time, you could find RV parks that cost about $5 a night. These days, though, you are going to come across those that easily hit the $40 per night mark. Make sure you are not under the false impression that RVing is going to be cheap simply because you did not get an expensive vehicle.

Myth #2: RV Costs Are Similar to Regular Vehicle Costs

When you are taking your RV for maintenance (or doing it yourself), it is not as easy as just popping open the hood and check to see if the brake fluid is looking good. The entire machinery of an RV is complex. The air conditioning system itself is much bigger than what you would find in a regular vehicle.

You are traveling with a portable home. There are going to be more costs involved than a simple four-wheel drive or sedan.

Even simply cleaning an RV is going to cost more since you have a bigger mode of transport (much bigger, to be honest) than a car. Think about this when you are purchasing your RV.

Myth #3: RVs Have a Lot of Storage Space

You are going to realize just how untrue this is when you actually enter an RV. This is the main reason why I have a separate chapter on downsizing, because I want people to be prepared before they step into an RV.

You cannot take anything and everything when you are in an RV. Sure, the bigger the RV, the more space you get to play around with, but that does not necessarily mean you should stuff in as many things as possible.

Myth #4: You Don't Have to Consider Safety During Purchase

This is wrong. Make sure you ask the dealer about the quality of the RV. In fact, make sure you are purchasing your RV from a trusted dealer. Or, in the case of a second-hand RV, make sure you are checking it for quality.

One of the things to consider is road vibration. As you are traveling, things get bounced around, including the entire frame of the RV. By making sure your purchase is made out of good materials, you can ensure its longevity. Don't skimp on your investment just to end up with a low-quality RV because of its price point.

Myth #5: I Made This Myth List to Scare You into Not Buying an RV

Absolutely not true. I truly want you to be part of this incredible life and wonderful journey I make with my own RV. But most of all, I want you to make an informed decision after considering all the facts and realities. I don't want you jumping to conclusions and regretting your investment later. Take your time to run through every factor before making the purchase of your RV. In fact, I recommend thinking things through even before you decide to downsize your home. And if you are already aware of all the points and myths, it doesn't hurt to think about them again.

Now, after you have thought about the points and myths, it is time to move on to the RV itself.

TYPES OF RVS

As you look around, you'll find different kinds of RVs available on the market based on size, features, and affordability. Here are their typical classifications:

Class-A: Motorhomes

Think about the mobile home bus of Will Smith, and you will then have a pretty good idea of what a Class-A RV looks like.

These RVs are the biggest things in the world and come with all the features that make it seem like you are traveling in a moving apartment. You typically do not find many second-hand or used Class-As on the road. That is simply because of the significant investment that goes into these RVs. You can find flat-screen TVs, ottomans, multiple sofas, large floor space, and a plethora of other features.

For Class-A trailers, here are some of the manufacturers you can look into:

- Newmar Corporation
- Tiffin Motorhomes
- Entegra Coach
- American Coach

Class-C: Motorhome

No, I have not made a mistake in the arrangement of the classes. Class-C is indeed much better than the Bs.

You can easily spot Class-Cs because they are typically built on the chassis of a van. In fact, one of their most notable features is the fact that their roof extends over the cab of the vehicle. Additionally, unless they have been repainted by the owners, they usually come in muted colors like grey, beige, dull white, and other similar shades.

These are cheaper than Class-As, and while they don't have all the technological marvels of Class-As, they do have an excellent balance of space and features for first time travelers.

For Class-C trailers, here are some of the manufacturers you can look into:

- Lazy Daze
- Winnebago Industries
- Dynamax
- Entegra Coach

Class-B: Motorhomes and Campervans

This entire class has a wide variety of options, all falling under the umbrella term of 'campervan.'

You can find large vans that have toilets and showers, or you could opt for the smaller vans with pop tops that look like they should be camped in at Woodstock. When you are looking at the bigger Class-Cs, you have RVs with enough space for one person to move from the front to the back of the van, with beds, stovetops, sinks, refrigerators, and other features to cater to your basic needs. But what they lack in space, they make up with one major advantage: they do not need a towing vehicle to move them around. They can also easily stop at many gas stations, unlike other forms of RVs.

For Class-B trailers, here are some of the manufacturers you can look into:

- Coach House
- Leisure Travel Vans
- Pleasure-Way Industries

School Buses

Seriously, school bus RVs are actually a thing!

There are many people who have opted to convert a school bus to a motorhome. The advantage is you can transform the interior in a manner that suits your preference. On the flipside, you have to either do all the work yourself, or pay someone to fix up the RV for you. You will also have to invest in all the materials needed for the RV.

Travel Trailers

The basic idea behind any travel trailer is that you attach a large living space to your truck or towing vehicle. They are usually compact, but you do have the option of making them larger. These are attached to the bumper of your towing vehicle. They also come in a few other options, which we are going to look at in the next few sections.

For your travel trailer requirements, here are some of the manufacturers you can look into:

- Outdoors RV
- Northwood Manufacturing
- Oliver Travel Trailers

Travel Trailers: Fifth Wheels

We've already discussed what fifth-wheel trailers are all about—they hook up to the bed of your truck. Fifth-wheel trailers can come in various sizes; they can be as large as Class-A motorhomes or they can be smaller than Class-Cs. It is all up to you. But do note that the bigger the trailer, the bigger (and more powerful) the towing vehicle you will need to pull it along.

For fifth-wheel trailers, here are some of the manufacturers you can look into:

- Outdoors RV
- New Horizons RV
- Northwood Manufacturing
- Grand Design RV

Travel Trailers: Teardrops

If you put Class-As on one end of the trailer spectrum, then teardrops fall on the other end. These regular-vehicle-sized trailers are the smallest option you can find. Some are made to include just a bedding space and are used primarily by people who want to have greater options when they are parking their vehicles. They are also easier to tow than other models of trailers.

For teardrop trailers, here are some of the manufacturers you can look into:

- nüCamp
- Little Guy Trailers

Travel Trailers: Pop Ups

What makes these trailers unique is that they can expand using tent sections and other kinds of 'pop ups.' These expansions are usually done to create more space for bedrooms and other facilities. Pop ups can have simple mechanisms, like tents, that give more room space and canopies that add shade outside the trailer. Or, they can have sections of the trailer that actually extend outwards to make more space. Not many people prefer to use pop ups, though, because of all the extra maintenance that goes into these and the fact that these RVs can be rather cumbersome for those who are planning to live in them. They are ideal for camping or short-term trips.

For pop up trailers, here are some of the manufacturers you can look into:

- Jayco
- Flagstaff
- LivinLite

Travel Trailers: Airstreams

These kinds of travel trailers are fairly easy to spot, as well. They usually have an aluminum body that is sometimes rounded. What they lack in space, they make up for in their build. They are solid and highly durable mobile homes. While they are usually smaller than regular sized fifth-wheels, they provide sturdiness that is not usually found in other trailers.

Airstreams are not just a type of trailer, but they are a brand, as well. Simply check out Airstream USA to see their range of travel trailers.

FLOOR PLANS TO THINK ABOUT

Here is the simple truth about floorplans: you can get one to fit any need, budget, or requirement. So don't worry if you feel like you are not going to get something that fits your tastes. When you are looking for the floor plan, there are three essential factors to consider.

Bed Space

If you are going to invest in a larger RV, you might not have a problem with bed space. However, if you do not have a lot of room, you will have to think about how you are going to fit in the bed. Many RVers find that placing the bed all the way in the back of the RV provides enough space in between for other amenities. But bedding ideas are entirely up to you.

Even if you are planning to get a spacious RV, think about the bed arrangement and how conveniently it can be accessed.

Bathroom Access

Where is the bathroom going to be? Is it going to be close to the bed? If that is the case, do you have enough space for a toilet and a shower? Would you like to add a sliding door or hinged door?

Think about the above questions as you plan out the bathroom space. When you are looking at different options of RVs, think about how these considerations can guide your purchasing decisions.

Refrigerator

If your RV comes with a refrigerator, then see if you are happy with where it is positioned or if you wish to make changes to it. In those cases where there is no refrigerator, you might have to go about installing one yourself. Measure the space where you are going to place your refrigerator to get a clear idea of the size of the refrigerator you will need. Look for any alternatives. Think about movement and proximity to other objects and doors.

Closet Space

Sometimes, having slides tend to block out access to the closets. In fact, you could even have a refrigerator whose doors could block you from reaching to other things. Some people are okay with such m nor inconveniences and learn to live in their RVs around these obstructions. If you think certain temporary blockages are workable, then you might have a certain degree of flexibility in choosing an RV. However, if you feel you need everything to be in its own space without preventing access to other areas of the RV, then you might have to think more carefully about how you are going to arrange things in your RV.

Work Space

Since you might be working from your RV, it may be a good idea to have a designated work space for yourself. Some people are comfortable spending a little extra to add in a work space, but if you are short on budget, consider turning one of the other spaces into a work space.

Alternatively, you can bring some foldable chairs and a table that you can set up outside your RV.

Dining Space

Some people are not picky about the dining space—they can turn any seated surface into a place to eat. However, if you have certain preferences, then make sure you are creating a space that fits well with your RV's floor plan. In Class-Cs and Class-Bs, you might end up making compromises with the space.

Space Jam!

In quite a few scenarios, you might not be able to get all the features crammed into your RV. If you do, then you may have a hard time accessing some of them. The space in your RV is going to be truly cramped, even closed off. The best way to decide how you would like to use the space is by listing the features that you want in your RV and that occupy the floor space. For example, let us assume that you have created the list below.

- Dining space
- Bathroom
- Refrigerator
- Work space
- Sofa area
- Recliner
- Fireplace

- Wardrobe

Your next step is to arrange them in the order of importance. Don't worry about adding features for aesthetic purposes right now—think of utility and usefulness. Let us now assume that after putting much thought into it, you have narrowed down the list to the below.

- Bathroom
- Refrigerator
- Dining space
- Work space
- Sofa area
- Wardrobe
- Fireplace
- Recliner

Start arranging the above features into your RV's space in the order of their appearance on the list. For example, you first measure the bathroom space and make sure that it is as close to your expectations as possible. Then, move on to the refrigerator and see if it fits well into your RV. Next, see if you have enough room for the dining space. If there is a special work space, that is an added bonus. At this point, you will have a clear idea of what you can do with the remaining floor space. Let's assume you have no space for a sofa, but can you add a small recliner instead? If not, perhaps an easy chair?

In such a manner, you can discover if there is enough space for the rest of the features on the list. Through efficient planning, you can have an RV that contains all your important needs within it, and if you do find some extra space, go right ahead and pack it with the additions you like!

LEARNING TO DRIVE YOUR RV

You might be wondering to yourself, why would I need to learn to drive a vehicle when I have been driving for X number of years?

The truth is that driving an RV is unlike operating any other vehicle you might have driven before. For that reason, here are a few simple tips you need to keep in mind before getting behind the steering wheel of your RV.

Tip #1: Start With the PMI

PMI stands for Preventative Maintenance Inspections. Check your tires, brakes, turn signals, the bulbs inside the RV, and other features so that you do not receive a nasty surprise while on the road.

Make sure you have clean linens on the bed and clean surfaces before you start out.

Check your inventory to see if you need to replenish anything, but most importantly, focus on the RV itself. You need to make sure everything is hazard-free before you move out.

Tip #2: *Understand Turning Radius*

When you turn, the radius taken by an RV is considerably greater than those taken by smaller vehicles. It is a good idea to identify the turn radius and keep it in mind before driving. Too often, people miscalculate because they suddenly realize they have been thinking about their four-wheel drive back at home, rather than their RV, which happens because of the long-time use of that familiar vehicle.

Tip #3: *Practice on Empty Roads*

Before you begin your adventure, make sure you have practiced driving your RV on empty roads. Check and see how easy it is to make turns. Get a feel for your RV so you can easily get yourself out of a jam when you encounter one.

Tip #4: Secure the Stuff in Your Motorhome

You do not want your cutlery flying around every time you make a turn in your RV. The best way to avoid that is by making sure you secure everything in your RV. If you need to use special locks or tags for that purpose, then do so before you head out.

Oh, and don't use your mobile phone while driving. Make sure that is secured somewhere, too, where it won't be a distraction to you while you're operating the vehicle.

Tip #5: Secure the Stuff Outside Your Motorhome

If you have objects attached to the outside of your motorhome, ensure that you have them tied down. You do not want that ladder attached to the back of your RV flying off and landing on top of the roof of someone else's car, making that person wonder if it has started raining stepladders all of a sudden.

For your own safety, and for the safety of others, make sure everything that could detach from the RV is fastened securely to the vehicle.

Tip #6: Maintain More Braking Distance

You are not racing anywhere, so make sure you maintain a safe braking distance from the vehicle in front of you. Ideally, you should be able to apply brakes well in advance, or at least give yourself the opportunity to slow down to a stop. Remember that your RV is probably packing more power than the vehicle in front of you.

Tip #7: Drive Slower

As I said, you are not racing anywhere. Drive slowly. Don't worry about people honking at you to go faster. Prudence is always the preferable option.

Think about it this way. If you are driving along a rather slippery road, then you need to have more control of your RV. The RV is a big machine, so if it loses traction on the road because you are driving too fast, then you are going to have an incredibly difficult time getting it back under control. Eventually, you will be involved in a fatal accident.

Instead, just keep calm and drive slowly.

Tip #8: Plan Your Route in Advance

Nothing ever goes perfectly. That is probably one of life's biggest principles. However, that does not mean you should leave everything to chance. Make sure you have a route planned out. That way, even if you have to divert, you have an idea of where to go back to.

Tip #9: Do Not Allow People to Walk Around While the RV is Moving

Encourage people to sit or lie down as much as possible. If anyone needs to use the facilities, let them know they should be doing so when you are on a relatively straight road and your speed is within a comfortable range.

This is another reason why you should drive slowly. If someone wants to use the bathroom while you are driving and you are going too fast and lose control of your RV, the bathroom is going to be a death trap for the people still inside.

Tip #10: Keep Your RV's Height in Mind

Certain underpasses and areas might have height limits. Make sure you know the height of your vehicle so you can navigate through them or, if you have to, around them using another access point.

Tip #11: Take Turns Slowly

Drive slow. Take turns slower.

There is no need to rush. Keep the turn radius in your mind when you are navigating turns. Remember your RV's height, as well, because as you turn, the center of gravity shifts. Your RV can tilt slightly and you might need to adjust the speed accordingly.

With all of the tips and recommendations in this chapter, you are ready for the RV lifestyle. Or are you? Perhaps you might have to consider a few more things before you shift to your motorhome.

CHAPTER 3
Transitioning into the RV Lifestyle

One does not simply pack everything and decide to shift to an RV lifestyle. You have to take a few things about your new mobile life into consideration.

There are certain mental, emotional, and logistical aspects to living in an RV. For example, if you are an introvert, how do you handle life on the road? What about a person who might experience claustrophobia when stuck in an enclosed space for too long? What happens if you are a social butterfly and would like to meet people on your journey?

Some people might think these questions above are rather trivial, but you need to understand them in order to have a sense of emotional and mental stability.

The first thing we are going to do in this chapter is discover how to have a fulfilling life within the RV lifestyle.

ADJUSTING TO YOUR NEW LIFE ON THE ROAD

There are a few things you need to remember before you start your journey, as well as certain factors to consider during your journey.

Think About Your Life Before Living It

It does not matter if you are planning to travel alone, with your pets, with friends, or with your family. Having a plan in mind helps you understand what you might need to do with certain components of the RV life. Here are a few questions for you to think about. You can add as many questions to the list below as you would like to get a full picture of your plan.

- What are you going to do with your residence once you have moved out? Are you planning to keep it locked, or would you like to entrust it to someone else?
- Do you have a way to earn income while on the road (more on this in a later chapter to

help give you ideas of income sources while you are on the road)?
- How are you going to stay connected?
- Are you comfortable living on backcountry areas and campgrounds, or are you only looking to stay in 5-star RV resorts?

Work Out a Rough Budget

You need to be aware of what kind of expenses you are going to have while you're traveling. In Chapter 1, we discovered how to establish a rudimentary budgeting system. Here, it's time to add in as many details as you would like so that you are completely aware of all the expenses you are going to incur on your journey.

You can also take this time to create your expected budget. This will help you understand just how much you are going to spend on a monthly basis, overall. You can then fix a number that will be your monthly limit. Having such a limit will prevent you from accidentally overspending.

Living the Lifestyle

You are transitioning from one lifestyle to the next. This means you are still going to have to perform your daily chores, run errands, pay bills, and engage in your usual activities. For this reason, you need to ask yourself if you are the kind of person who prefers to stay in a particular location for a while, or if you would like to constantly move from one place to another. Are you comfortable boondocking out in the national forests, or are you only interested in using campgrounds?

By knowing your travel style, you might gain a better idea of how you are going to take care of your daily tasks and find time for your work and other projects.

HOW TO SURVIVE LIVING IN A SMALL SPACE!

Once you have decided to live in an RV, it is not just about taking care of your daily needs, but also about making the most out of a tiny space. How can one do it? What should one remember when living in such a small area?

Multi-Purpose Spaces

Since you are not going to have a lot of space for everything, you should think about how you are going to use existing surfaces for various purposes. For example, your dining table could serve as your work space and for preparing your meals.

You might also have to put many items in one spot. Often, you might find that your laptop and work tech will be sharing space with your groceries and other random items. Be prepared for this, and even try to think about ways you can create spaces that can be used for many purposes.

Make Time for the Outdoors

Living in a small space means you are not going to get a lot of natural light. Even if you have windows, you might not receive the required amount of natural light to maintain your health. Take time to step outside and enjoy the outdoors. This could also be the perfect time to pick up some healthy habits, such as walking or jogging. Whatever it may be, it will allow you to explore the world outside, get some fresh air, and even flex your muscles.

Besides, you might need to stretch our legs once in a while, so why not do it through an activity?

Learn to Cook Simple Meals

Sometimes, you won't have the opportunity to prepare a fancy five-course meal, especially when you are driving for long hours. This is why it's a good idea to try and learn quick one-pot meals. There are so many options available online to offer you variety and they don't take too much time to prepare.

However, this does not mean you can never prepare a nice dinner or a wonderful breakfast, but it is better to know how to cook different kinds of meals so you are prepared for any occasion. For example, let's say you are running out of supplies and you still have a day to go before you can restock. By knowing how to cook a nice and simple meal, you can make use of what you have to the fullest.

Meet People

If you are a person who enjoys social interaction, then get to know people when you park your RV at campgrounds or other places, if you have the opportunity. Also, do not lose touch with the people who matter in your life back at home. Contact your friends and family as frequently as you can so you do not feel a sense of loneliness as you travel the road.

Get a Pet

Pets are a great addition to the RV, if you have the space for them. Make sure your pet can easily fit within the vehicle, and that they are comfortable and fed properly. During my journeys, I have come across quite an interesting collection of pets, including a goat, owl, pig, gecko, and even a parrot. Of course, most of these people were either traveling alone or in pairs. Some had their families with them, but they were efficient in the way they managed their RVs and pets.

Pets are truly wonderful companions. Make sure you have your RV prepared for them and, more importantly, make sure they are RV-ready. For example, you cannot think about getting huskies in your RV. These dogs are hyperactive and require a lot of activity during the day. Know your RV before you get your pet.

The Dirty Stuff

Sometimes, you are going to be carrying dirt from the outdoors into your RV. Make sure you have a system in place to deal with that. For example, you can put a mat outside and ask people to remove their shoes before they enter the vehicle. Or, you can sweep the RV twice a day to ensure that people do not spread the dirt everywhere. Ideally, I think it would be better if you try and ensure that your RV is a no-footwear zone (except perhaps near the entrance).

Cables

It is always useful to have extension cords so you can charge your devices, however, this could lead to wire clutter. Make sure you are putting away your chargers and other wires when you are done using them. This not only allows others to use the extension cords, but also keeps your RV tidy.

Have a Comfortable Routine

An RV is a small space. This means you are going to create noise and interruptions, even when you do not want to. This might become obvious when you have others traveling with you. If you notice others sleeping or resting, then try to minimize your noise as much as possible. In fact, try to establish a routine where everyone can get some quiet time if they need it.

Clean Up

Try to establish frequent cleaning routines. When your space looks clean, it sometimes does not matter if it is small or big. Make sure you have healthy habits, such as cleaning up after you eat, keeping everything tidy and the floors swept, and maintaining the RV itself so it looks clean on the outside. Of course, cleaning an RV is a much longer process, so you don't have to do this every day. But keep a routine so you don't forget to give your motorhome some cleaning every so often.

Keep Things Organized

Have a spot for everything you own. Do not throw things in random places. Organizing helps you in two ways:

- It keeps the interior of the RV neat and tidy.
- You are able to find things when you need them. You might think things won't get misplaced in such a small space, but they can, and you could end up spending some time trying to recover them.

Keep Bedding Simple

This might sound like a rather odd point to make, but when you add too many items on your bed, it tends to make the space look smaller. Use plain colors and avoid placing too many cushions and objects on the bed. This way, the space appears considerably bigger.

Perform Regular Maintenance

Your RV comes with a water system and probably an air conditioning system. Since it might be pretty expensive to take care of things in the long run, make sure you are maintaining them as much as possible.

To do this, try to learn more about your RV. You can ask for help from the RV dealership, from local RVers, or you could find plenty of useful information online. No matter what your problem is, chances are there is a solution in the world of the internet.

TRAVELING WITH KIDS AND ANIMALS

To better deal with this section, let's split them into two. We are going to first focus on RVing with your kids, and then move on to pets.

Tips for RVing With Your Kids

Get the Right RV

This is probably self-explanatory, but make sure your RV is appropriate for your kids. Typically, when you are getting your RV, you will be told how many people the RV is ideal for. Some RVs are good for three to four people, while others give a wider option with two to seven people. Knowing this will help you decide which motorhome will give you as much comfort as possible during your travels.

Plan the Trip in Advance

It is fun to be spontaneous, and while you can still do that, it is always better to have a rough plan for your travels. This allows you to determine specific stops for taking a break, having food, using the facilities, restocking certain items, or simply allowing the kids to experience the outdoors for a bit.

Even if you would prefer not to have a plan, make sure you have a map or guide with the locations of important places. These could include gas stations, campgrounds, parks, and other areas for your RV. This way, even if you need to make an emergency stop for any reason, you can quickly refer to your map and find the closest campground or RV spot for your motorhome.

You can even get some incredible RV apps to help you plan your journey or guide you towards the nearest essential spot.

Check out some of these apps:

- InRoute Route Planner
- Roadtrippers
- Google Trips

I would also recommend the following navigation app:

- CoPilot RV: I like this app since you can actually use it offline! The best part is you can enter in your RV's height and width, and it will calculate the best route to reach a specific location without running into low bridges and tight tunnels—definitely something that might be useful when you don't have the best internet connection.

These apps give you added benefits or make your trip more interesting:

- Gas Buddy: If you don't just want to know where the nearest gas station is, but where the cheapest one is, then you need this app.

- TuneIn Radio: You get to tune in to local radio stations for news or your favorite sport updates.

For finding spots for camping, you can use the below apps:

- Reserve America
- Recreation.gov
- iOverlander
- Campendium

Stay Updated

Try to keep yourself informed about the latest news and information for the areas you are in. This helps you find out weather updates and other details that could be useful for your travels—for example, finding out there is construction coming up on one of the highways you have been traveling on could give you the idea to try an alternative route. The same goes for the weather and local news. Here are some options you can look into:

- TuneIn Radio
- NPR One
- Pandora

Pack Lightly

One mistake most people make is that they try to cram as many clothes and other objects into their suitcases as possible. But you won't be needing all those clothes, and they only end up taking valuable space you could have used for something else.

Make sure you travel light. Remember the list we made in the chapter on downsizing? Stick to that. Also, make sure you use soft luggage as it will not only help prevent any injuries (as with hard luggage), but you might also be able to squeeze them together more efficiently in tight spaces. Hard luggage tends to take up more space, and there is nothing you can do to make them occupy a smaller space.

Ban the Electronics

Make the trip all about the trip.

Removing electronic devices allows you to connect with your kids and gives you the opportunity to experience the journey with them without any distractions. Additionally, you are going to save a lot of electricity in the RV (and eventually fuel costs) by minimizing electronics as much as possible.

Keep Portable Snacks

Sometimes, you might need to travel for a fair amount of time before you reach a particular camp. Additionally, you may not be able to make multiple emergency stops every time your kids might get hungry as you might disrupt traffic, or there may not be any place to park your RV.

To deal with such scenarios, make sure you pack snacks in portable containers. By doing so, you won't have to worry about making emergency stops to eat a quick bite.

Don't Drive Every Day

Even if you are planning to travel consistently, make sure you plan stops for a few days at a time. This allows you to unwind and perform important chores in the RV, while also giving the kids a chance to head outside. Small breaks such as these allow you to relax both physically and mentally.

You don't have to be in a hurry to get anywhere. The main purpose of having an RV lifestyle is to attain a sense of fulfillment. That might not happen if you are constantly moving around without a break.

BBQ Nights and S'mores

Make your RV trip fun. Have BBQ nights and enjoy some s'mores by the fire. Play fun games with your kids. Take them out trekking on adventures. You'll not only bond well with your children, but they'll have a lot of fun while on the trip!

I mean, thinking about the next stop and planning camping is all well and good, but what's the point if you are not having fun?!

Try to Avoid Extreme Temperatures

This is where the need to stay informed comes in. While you might have the immune system of the Incredible Hulk, the same cannot be said about your children, so try to avoid places with extreme temperatures or temperature fluctuations.

Or, in other words, stay updated!

TIPS FOR RVING WITH PETS

Rules of the Road

While it might seem rather natural to allow your pets to roam around the RV while you are driving, it could actually be dangerous for both you and the pet (and the RV, of course).

While you might be following the speed limits, the same cannot be said about other drivers. You will need to keep your eyes on the road to deal with any troublesome motorists. But even if you are on an empty stretch of road, wandering pets tend to cause distractions, which is something you shouldn't have to worry about when driving.

Pack the Essentials

When in doubt, make a list.

Get all the essentials for your pet. Here is a list I made to give you a little guidance on what you should include, but feel free to modify it as you see fit:

- Leash
- Crates
- Litter
- Toys
- Pet carriers
- Refuse bags for pet droppings
- Brush and grooming items

I know, a lot of people might frown upon the idea of putting their pets in carriers, but think about what matters most: a temporary safe enclosure for your pet, or a potential accident waiting to happen?

Update Your Pet IDs and Bring Them With You

As with the list you made during the downsizing process, make sure you get the actual IDs of your pets. Make a few copies and also save them virtually.

Add Exercise as Your Daily Habit

Moving around your muscles and body from time to time is not just healthy for you, but your pet as well. As we discussed in the section about RVing with your kids, try not to drive every day. Stop for a while at camps and take your pet out for walks. If your pet is a bird, you might want to keep it outdoors for a while. Of course, you might also want to keep it on a leash if you are worried that your bird might fly away.

Get a Pet Bathing Kit

Many people often overlook this part and end up giving their pet baths using the bathroom or the water hose (which is not the ideal way to clean your pet). Make space for a bathing kit for your pet so you are not wondering where the nearest pool with clear water is.

MAKING YOUR RV FEEL LIKE HOME

Home is where the heart is, even if said home is moving around a lot.

People often wonder if they can make their RV feel a little more like the home they've left behind. It is definitely possible, and I am going to show you how.

Home Tip #1: Change the RV Mattress

The mattress that comes with your RV might not be suitable for you, so make sure you change it to something a bit more comfortable. If you feel that getting a brand-new mattress is not something you would like to invest in, there are cheaper alternatives. For one, you can get a mattress topper, which is essentially a layer of bedding you add on top of your mattress. Alternatively, you could even take the mattress from your home and put it in your RV if the mattress can fit on the RV's bed.

Home Tip #2: Add Wall Decor

Include pictures, stickers, or other wall decorations to bring a little color and life to your RV. Adding wall clocks showing times from different parts of the world is also a wonderful addition.

Here are some other ideas you can consider:

- A map of the country or region
- Photo frames containing fun sayings or messages
- Hanging pots and plants (make sure they are completely secure, or you could choose artificial plants, as well). HINT: You can choose to take down the pots and plants when you are traveling and set them up again after you have parked your RV, but that means you have to manage your space very well since these decorative items can take up a lot of space.
- LED lights
- Flameless candles (they set the ambience without setting your RV on fire)
- Hanging wicker baskets is a great idea for décor and storage

Home Tip #3: Use Oil Diffuser

Get your RV smelling fresh. It doesn't take too long for the RV to accumulate a plethora of scents from your travels. Using an oil diffuser can make all the difference in the world. Scents such as eucalyptus add a little freshness into the air, while rose can provide a wonderful sweet smell. Look at different oils and find the one that suits you. If you are traveling with other people, let them smell the scents before you buy them so you can find out if anyone is allergic to the fragrance.

Home Tip #4: Home Comforts

Remember how we talked about bringing bathroom slippers and cutlery? Many people prefer to buy new items for the RV, but I like to have things from my home because they make the RV feel lived in. Bring in your favorite coffee mug. Get your comfortable home slippers. Add your welcome mats, if you would like. Things you have already used before entering your RV have a sense of value to them, and bringing them to your RV transfers that value to your motorhome.

Home Tip #5: Add Curtains

If your RV comes with valences, then see if you can replace them with curtains. With such a simple addition, the interior of your RV transforms into something comfortable and cozy.

Home Tip #6: Bring Your Favorite Tunes

I am serious. Playing your favorite music in the RV can actually make a whole lot of difference.

Let me give you an example.

If you had a particular playlist you used to play while working from home, then playing that playlist in your RV can actually make you feel like you are once again working from home.

But there are other situations where music could very well be the remedy. You are going to face some challenges while RVing—perhaps it could begin to rain heavily and you might have to stop for a while until the weather changes for the better. You are unable to do anything but sit and wait out the downpour. During those times, think about the moments when you used to play your favorite songs at home, the ones you or your entire family would enjoy. Perhaps you and your family used to take turns playing music because one person could not decide whose music was better until, eventually, everyone decided they should each have a turn at picking a track.

Recreate the same experience in your RV. Either put on a nice playlist or let people take turns playing some of their favorite songs.

Allow for this experience to happen not just during a chaotic situation, but for other times as well. Enjoy your favorite music and the preferred music of your passengers whenever they are in the mood, just like you would at home.

Home Tip #7: The Great Outdoors

Just because you have an RV does not mean you cannot extend your home space to the great outdoors. In fact, that is one of the benefits of having such a vehicle. You can have so many unique outdoor vistas, locations, and sights to experience.

To do this, see if you have enough space to pack an outdoor tent. In fact, if you are staying at a particular spot for a few days, you can even use the tent as an extension of your living space. Toss in a mat and a few cushions and you could work, relax, or just have fun outside.

Home Tip #8: Keep Things Neat and Organized

I've already made a point about this, but it requires mentioning again because this time, it concerns the environment you are trying to maintain. Clutter not only disrupts the homey atmosphere you are trying to establish, but also has an impact on your mind. More clutter makes your space feel untidy and creates a sense of chaos, subconsciously creating a sense of chaos in your mind as well.

Have you ever been in the middle of a traffic jam and felt the stress it gives you? Now think back to those times you were in the presence of nature, where there were not a lot of people around and you felt peaceful and serene.

The same situation applies here. When you are in the presence of cutter and chaos, your mind reacts to it accordingly. If there is a sense of order and tidiness, however, your mind itself begins to project order and tidiness into your life.

With the above tips, you have made a wonderful transition to your RV lifestyle, but transitioning is only the first step. Now you have to start living in your RV and take care of it. For that, we move on to Chapter 4.

CHAPTER 4
What You Need to Know Before You Go!

THE PREPARATIONS ARE complete. The plans have been set. You are certain that you have looked into everything. The time has come for you to begin your journey.

But as you are journeying in your RV, there are a few things you need to keep in mind, especially when it comes to the maintenance of your motorhome.

HOW DO YOU DUMP THE TANKS?

Cleaning the RV holding tanks is not a job anyone would willingly take. However, it has to be done and you have to dispose of the human waste in a proper manner (while taking care to not disturb the environment).

There are some simple steps to take care of the tanks, but before we start doing that, let's see what we might need in order to prepare ourselves.

Prepping With the Right Tools

You will need the following tools before you start dumping anything out of your RV:

- Disposable gloves
- Rinse hose to flush out the black water
- Bleach wipes for sanitation
- Clear sewer adaptor
- Sewer extension hose (ideally 30 feet long)
- Hose elbow
- Hand sanitizer to clean your hands after you are done

Types of RV Tanks

Depending on how your RV has been set up, you might find the below tanks attached to your motorhome:

- Black tank to take care of the wastewater and sewage from your toilet
- Grey tank to deal with the water from your shower and sinks

- Freshwater tank that stores clean water (this is the water you use in the shower and sinks)

We are going to start by learning how to empty the black water tank first.

Waste Disposal

Ideally, look for RV dump stations and other designated areas for taking care of the black water tank. These areas and installations are specially-made to provide you with the convenience of cleaning out your tanks in a safe, sanitary manner. Once you have located these tanks, follow the process below:

1. Put on your gloves and make sure there are no tears in the fabric. Make sure the valves of the grey and black tanks are closed before you move on to the next step.
2. Now start by attaching one end of the hose to the sewer or dump station hole. You can also make use of a hose elbow and a hose ring to connect the hose properly to the dump station or sewer hole. By doing so, you can attach the hose securely. However, this is not always needed if you are careful when getting rid of the waste. Also, don't just leave your hose lying around when you are draining

your RV. Make sure you are either holding it or securing it using the elbow and hose ring. Even with additional measures to secure the hose, it is still prudent to hold the hose in case there is an unexpected disaster and you need to react quickly.

3. Connect the other end of the hose to the black water tank. You might think people are careful when it comes to attaching their hoses, but you would be surprised by how many people do not double check to make sure everything has been fastened. One way to connect the hose to the tank is by first positioning the opening underneath the black tank outlet. Once done, open the flap and allow any drips to fall directly into the hose. When you notice the drips have stopped entirely, connect the hose to the tank and secure it properly.

4. When you are confident that everything is properly attached, open the black tank water valve first. You will hear the noise of wastage rushing through the hose. Eventually, you will start to hear a trickling sound.

5. Do not remove the hose yet. Flush the black tank with water to clean it completely. Certain RVs have the ability to use the clean water

from the grey water tank to perform this task. If not, you might have a different setup to help you with this process. Typically, you might also have a rinse system in the RV that you can connect to the black tank. Fill the tank up to two-thirds with water and then flush out the tank once again. This will allow you to clean the tank, as well as the hose.
6. Make sure you close the valve to your black water tank.
7. When you are done, remove the end of the hose that is connected to the tank first. Lift it up so you can drain any leftover materials from the pipe straight down into the dump station or sewer hole. If you have a separate hose for cleaning, use that to clean the hose instead.
8. Finally, detach the end of the hose connected to the dump station or sewer hole.
9. Repeat steps 2 through 8 for the grey water tank.

The Dumping of the Dump Stations

One of the things people have begun to notice is that RV dump stations are slowly disappearing. This is because people are not careful when they are cleaning out their RVs; they simply don't care about spillage, or they misuse the facilities.

When you are using a dump station, make sure you are following proper etiquette.

- The dump stations are only meant for the contents of your holding tank. Don't throw anything else in there.
- If you accidentally make a mess or spill something, be respectful and courteous—clean up after yourself!
- Do not dump garbage or trash in the area. Find designated spots to discard any other form of waste materials.
- Do not discard your gloves or any other equipment into the sewer hole.
- Most dump stations or sewer holes come with a flap or covering. Make sure you close them. You don't have to leave it open for the next person.
- Don't use the dump stations to simply park your RV while you begin to clean other materials and objects. Leave it open for the next traveler to use.

Cleaning the Tanks

You have successfully emptied the tanks. But what about the tanks themselves? How can you make sure they are clean?

Here are a few ways to take care of your tank.

Once you have dumped your tanks, you can then use tank treatments (one such example is the RV Digest-It). All you have to do is pour it down your toilet. It removes any foul smell and also helps in digesting the waste quickly. It is recommended that you use treatment products frequently, as this helps in avoiding any clogs or waste build-up in the tank.

There are also items called cleaning wands that help you clean out the tank more effectively. Connect them to any garden hose and you can then use them to dislodge any waste materials from your RV tank.

Arranging the Waste Equipment

Make sure any items that are used for waste disposal are kept separately from other items in your RV. You might also need to clean these materials.

Make sure you strap on your rubber gloves and use a cleaning solvent or solution for the purpose.

You can also sanitize the items by taking a large bucket and filling it with water. Add in a solution of bleach (usually at the rate of ¼ cup for every gallon of water). Soak the items inside the solution for at least four hours. You don't have to do this frequently—if you can perform this just once a month, you are good to go. You can also do this before the start of each season.

Additional Help

One of the apps I think you might find invaluable is the Sanidumps RV Dump Station Locator. This app allows you to find the closest dump station. All the results you look for are located on Google Maps, allowing you to easily find navigable routes towards that particular dump station. A lot of people might not think of how useful this app is until they are left searching for the nearest dump station.

REGULAR MAINTENANCE ON THE ROAD

Just like your tank, your RV is going to need some maintenance as well. To a lot of people, this might seem like an overwhelming task since they are often left wondering what part of the RV they should start working on first.

Here is a list to get you started.

Maintenance #1: Look at the Seams and Seals of the RV

Use your ladder (or some other way) to inspect the roof of your RV. Check for any leakages that could let rainwater into the interior of the vehicle. Check the skylights, vents, edges, and air conditioning unit. If you notice any leaks, you can make use of any number of sealants available in the market. However, try to choose a sealant that works well with the material your RV is made of. Think about getting the gaps or holes fixed sometime in the near future to provide a more long-term solution to the problem.

Maintenance #2: Check Your Tire Pressure and Wheel Nuts

Your RV's tires are going to suffer quite a bit of abuse (not to mention with the weight of the RV on them). Make sure you are checking the air pressure in your wheels to maintain safety on the road. Look at the lug nuts to see if any of them have come loose, even just a little, and make sure the tires are not overinflated. This could cause them to explode, leading to some serious accidents on the road. The seasons affect the tire pressure, as well. For example, if you are planning to spend time in a particular location during winter, make sure you check your tires before heading out because tire pressure can drop significantly during this time of year.

Maintenance #3: Check the Batteries

Your aim with the batteries is to keep them fully charged, but people don't always pay attention to that as it means making frequent trips to the garage. However, what you can do is make sure the batteries are in good condition before your long trips.

Maintenance #4: Maintain Your RV's Tanks

We had already seen a step-by-step process of how you can maintain the tanks of your RV. Do not leave your RV tanks uncleaned or undrained for a long time. There are numerous products that can help you with tank treatment. Here are some products that have received some good reviews:

- Happy Campers Organic RV Holding Tank Treatment
- Rid-X RV Toilet Treatment Liquid
- Walex TOI-91799 Porta-Pak Holding Tank Deodorizer

These are just some of the products on the market you can make use of. Whether you would like to remove odor or dislodge waste materials, there is a product out there for you.

Maintenance #5: Keep Your RV's Brakes Maintained

Check out the wheel bearings and other brake parts to ensure they are well lubricated. Brake repairs can be rather expensive, so frequent maintenance can help you avoid shelling out hundreds of dollars for a replacement.

Maintenance #6: Check Your RV's Slide-Outs

If your RV comes with many parts that can slide out, then make sure you check them regularly, especially their seams and seals. If you notice dust or other particles, clean them out so you don't have any obstructions causing further damage.

Maintenance #7: Replace the Fuel, Coolant, Air, and Hydraulic Filters in Your RV

The first thing you have to do before you even think about replacing anything is to check the current condition of the parts. Look at the fuel, coolant, air, and hydraulic filters to see if they need a bit of cleaning. Do not take any chances if you see them ruined beyond repair.

Maintenance #8: Towing Vehicle Connection

Some people establish an electrical connection between the towing vehicle and the trailer. If you do, make sure this connection is working properly without a hitch. This connection is useful for various reasons. One of them is the fact that when you hit the brakes, the brake lights on the trailer will light up. The same goes for the signal indicator as well.

WHY YOUR RV NEEDS TO BE LEVEL

Often, people don't think about leveling their RV, but this is an important part of taking care of your motorhome. It doesn't matter if you are looking to camp somewhere temporarily or if you are planning to use the RV as a new home, leveling helps you make the most of some of the RV's features.

If you don't level your RV, you might experience one (or all) of the below problems.

Warm Refrigerator

You wake up one morning to the smell of freshness in the air. A nice breakfast would be perfect. So you head out to the refrigerator to get your ingredients. However, as soon as you open the door, you notice the food has spoiled. What's more, the beer is warm as coffee (the horror!).

What just happened? The refrigerator was working perfectly yesterday. In fact, you can still taste the lingering flavor of the nice, chilled beer you were enjoying just last night.

Time for a bit of science. Liquid ammonia flows through a part of the evaporator coils inside the refrigerator, which are usually at low temperatures. But one of the key components to keep this process going is gravity. As you probably already know, liquids don't go uphill (if it does, then you have discovered something magnificent). If your RV is uneven, one side of the refrigerator is tilted upwards, preventing the liquid from reaching that place. The ammonia can actually pool and settle, causing a blockage in your refrigerator. If you continue to operate your refrigerator at an uneven level, especially for a prolonged period of time, you may be hit with an expensive repair bill (which, when combined with a warm beer, is a recipe for a bad mood).

You can use a spirit level to check for any tilts. You might already know about these handy tools. They usually have a liquid inside them that is often green in color. There is a bubble that goes from one side to the next and if that bubble remains in the center, then the object or space is leveled properly.

Note that some of the newer models of refrigerators function much better than the older ones, but leveling is almost always beneficial to your RV's refrigerator.

Things Not Staying in One Spot

Being on level ground means you have level countertops and objects are not moving from one end to the other inside the RV. Objects won't fall over or fly around in the RV, especially if they are mounted (which can make for some rather deadly projectiles). With a surface that is not level, you might be fighting to keep the coffee mug from sliding off the table, having a nice meal with the food looking like it wants to escape from your plate, and other such inconveniences.

Lack of Sleep

When the RV is not leveled, you might find it difficult to get a good night's sleep. We are used to sleeping on level ground and a tilted level feels alien to us. Plus, there is the problem of rolling off your bed, into the wall, into another person, or just moving around as though your body is somehow figure skating in your sleep. None of the aforementioned situations sound like they could contribute to a blissful sleep.

Wrong Water Tank Levels

Most RVs come with water tank readers that let you know the current level of your water. With a tilt, they could show a shortage of water, sending you into panic mode because you just filled the freshwater tank recently. Now, you are needlessly worried about a possible leak in the tank or that you hadn't actually bought enough water.

Damage to the Slide-Outs

People often think slide-outs are sturdy and strong. While that may be true, they are still affected by the same forces that made the apple fall from the tree into Newton's lap. Yes, we are talking about gravity. Fun fact: the whole scenario of Newton sitting under the apple tree and discovering gravity is a myth.

But back to the point I am trying to make. If the RV is not level, the slide-outs will apply pressure on one side of the RV. This causes damage to that side, affecting the mechanisms that operate the slide-outs.

WHAT TO DO IF THE RV BREAKS DOWN

Spending a night stranded on the side of the road does not contribute to the adventure you had planned for yourself or your family, which is why you should keep the below tips in mind.

Prevention Is Better Than Repair

Make sure you are performing routine maintenance and check-ups on your RV. Do not leave your motorhome unattended for a long time. Through check-ups, you can discover any problem before it worsens. You must be aggressive when you are working on preventive care. It's either that, or looking embarrassingly in your side mirror as your RV is billowing smoke through a nice neighborhood and the folks nearby are throwing some rather colorful language your way. In all honesty, a broken-down RV is a danger to you, as well as the people who are in close proximity to the vehicle.

When Trouble Comes Knocking at the Door

In a perfect world, inspections are all it takes to keep trouble at bay, but we are not in a perfect world and, well, excrement happens (this is strictly a PG-13 book). Here, we are going to assume the inevitable has happened. So what do you do? How can you deal with the scenario?

If a breakdown occurs, it could happen in any form ranging from an empty gas tank to a wobbly wire to other mechanical failures indicated by terrifying noises you know should not be coming out of any vehicle, let alone one you live in. In such cases, if you can keep driving, then do so until you have reached a safe place to park your motorhome, whether that place is a truck shop, RV camp, or a wide open space. During this process, take it slow. Put on your hazard lights and move to one side of the road, allowing the traffic to pass you by. If you start smelling something funky, make sure you find a spot to pull over as quickly as possible.

Keep your RV as far off the road as possible without tipping it over into a ravine or getting the tires stuck in soft mud. If you have people with you and they look at you with expressions of concern, stay calm. This will assure them there is nothing major to be concerned about.

Do the traffic a favor and set up cones or reflector triangles to divert them to a safer lane. You can also use flares for this purpose, but if there is an oil leak, skip this step.

Do your family a favor by not getting run over while you are setting up stuff on the road.

Keep the hazard lights on and if you have some reflective clothing, put it on. Have some for your family and make them wear it as well.

Once you have ensured the RV is parked to the side of the road and you, your family, and your pets are all safe, you can then call for backup. If you are one of those people who has spent considerable time in the garage, you might already know what to do about the problem. But, like most of us, you might be out-matched by the complexity of the problem. In this case, don't try and fix anything yourself. Let the help arrive and take over.

Calling Support

Remember when I mentioned a few apps you should have with you? Well, make sure that along with those apps, you also have the phone numbers and contact details of nearby RV assistance programs or establishments.

On the off-chance that you cannot find the number of the local help, then either call 9-1-1 if there is an emergency, or take a cab to the nearest town to look for support. If you can find a gas or service station nearby, reach out to them for help. Usually, if the problem is small, then they might be able to take care of it easily.

You could also sign up for roadside assistance or RV insurance, which we shall look at a later chapter. However, keep in mind something important—make sure that when you are signing up for such roadside assistance, you check the below criteria:

- They have nationwide coverage
- They have the type of towing facilities that can tow the RV you have. Imagine signing up for assistance and realizing they can't tow your RV for repairs—that's going to be a bummer.

Service Centers

Now, let us suppose that you have not signed up for any assistance. This is where connectivity comes in as you can easily look online for the nearest service center.

If connectivity is an issue in the area you're visiting, make sure you have saved the numbers of all the essential service centers along the roads you are taking. This technique of saving the numbers of service centers works both for when you have a planned journey, as well as if you are being spontaneous. Here's why:

If your journey is planned, then all you have to do is store the numbers beforehand.

If you are trying to be spontaneous, you still typically decide where to go before you get into the RV. Whenever you choose your destination, quickly check online for all the service centers along the way and make a note of their contact details before hitting the road.

But honestly, I prefer that you are always prepared for any emergency. Keep contacts of these service centers or repair shops so you are not left stranded in the middle of an empty highway—that looks like it could be the setting for a new horror show—without any idea of what to do next.

ELECTRICITY AND POWER

Most of us here aren't electrical engineers. However, if you just so happen to be one, you might be tempted to skip this chapter with a confident smile on your face, thinking, "Pfft! I already know whatever he is about to say."

However, I still recommend you read this chapter so you can understand the basics of RV electricity and power, and how your expertise can be put to use.

Importance of Power

Essentially, one of the things you should remember when you are thinking about your RV's power is a formula: watts, which signifies the total power, is a result of current, the product of amps and volts. If you transfer the statement into an equation, it's written as: watts = amps x volts, or $W = A \times V$.

The above formula will help you manage the number of electrical devices you have plugged in at any point in your RV. You could potentially use all the electrical devices you have, as long as they are within the limit of the total wattage. However, if you cross the limit, then you might just trip the circuit. That means interrupting a plot twist in the movie you were watching in the RV—definitely not something you would want to happen.

Read up about the total wattage of your RV. You can find this information in your vehicle's manual. When you are using electrical appliances, check how much power is needed for each appliance. This way, you can find out if you have to turn off some electrical devices before plugging in another. You really don't want your RV to shut down because you were making coffee.

One for Two

Your RV comes with two different types of electrical systems:

- A 12-volt electrical system
- A 120-volt electrical system

The 12-volt electrical system is typically powered by a single battery, but that may not be the case as some RVs have multiple batteries powering the system. This system is responsible for running your refrigerator, your water heater, your water pump, most of the lights in your RV, and many other vital components. The 120-volt electrical system, on the other hand, is used for other devices plugged into outlets, such as the television, kitchen appliances, phone chargers, or computer power cords. The 120-volt system is usually powered by a generator.

In the end, both systems need to be charged whenever you get the opportunity. But how can you charge them? It all comes down to the power cord.

30 Amp or 50 Amp

Most RVs come with a power cord you can use to plug in to an electrical charging outlet, which can be found at most camps. The cords come in two forms, 30-amp and 50-amp.

A 30-amp power cord has three prongs and the 50-amp comes with four. At this point, the statement "the more the merrier" couldn't be truer. The 50-amp cord, with its four prongs, provides more power than a 30-amp cord.

When you enter an RV campground, you might be able to find a charging station for both the 30-amp and 50-amp cord types. But in many camps, there may not be an option for the 50. It is for this reason that I recommend having an adapter to convert a 50-amp to a 30-amp. However, if you are using an adapter, be aware of an important point. Even though you are using a 50, converting it into a 30-amp cord means you are generally going to get the same power a 30 does, rather than getting the entire power of the 50. This is why it is always prudent to make a note of your electrical appliances and gadgets. You can find out how to use them in any situation you are presented with.

Don't Just Plug In

Your phone or laptop has been switched off for a long time. You cannot wait to get them both started so you can access your work, visit your social platforms for a quick update, or just know you are still connected to the Internet. You spot a camp, and in that camp, you see the charging station. At that point, you know how the people who first discovered fire might have felt.

So you park your RV and get the plug out to charge your vehicle.

But hold on there just a minute. There are a few things you need to know before you plug in.

- First, check if the campground's electrical wiring is safe. The easiest way to do this is by using a polarity tester. You can find these relatively inexpensive devices at most electrical stores. The polarity tester will let you know if there is a potential for any or all of the electrical components of your RV to get fried.
- Next, make sure you switch off all electricity in your RV.
- Once you have done that, you can then plug in the power cord. Make sure the connection is secure before you switch on the charge.
- If you have the budget, you can consider investing in surge guards. They are an extra precaution against a sudden surge of power to your systems.
- Finally, you can start charging your RV.

Solar Power

Those who have the necessary investment capabilities may want to think about using solar panels to power the RV. However, make sure you are aware of the weather in your area. If you have sufficient sunlight, adding solar panels might benefit you.

Many RVers who enjoy boondocking or camping in the wilderness where there are no charging capabilities often make use of solar panels to supply their vehicles with the required power.

RV Insurance

Stuff happens. And when you have coverage, you can turn to your insurance company to take care of the necessary expenses. The question is, how do you choose the best insurance for your RV? What companies should you trust?

Here are a few tips to keep in mind when checking out the insurance:

- Take your time when you are looking for insurance. You can go directly to an insurance company to ask for more details, as well as look for specialty brokers or agents. They have a wealth of information that can help you be sure of your decision. Check online for

reviews about insurance companies, however, note that people often give low reviews because they are either disgruntled or they did not read the fine print before signing on for something. Find other sources of information to learn more about RV insurance companies even if you have to seek advice from your friends or family who might have knowledge about this topic. In fact, try to get in touch with the RV community. Word-of-mouth information is valuable and might point you in the right direction.
- Make sure you and the insurance company have the same value for your RV before you buy the insurance. This ensures that if a loss does occur at some point, the cash value the insurance company places on your RV aligns with what you had in mind.
- Double and triple check all the coverage you are getting. You don't want to buy insurance and then later realize some parts are missing. Also, look for any additional benefits provided by the company or institution.
- Many insurers will adjust your premium based on where you store your RV. Make sure you have stored your RV in a safe environment,

and do not lie about this to your insurance company.

- If you have a decent no-claims bonus on an existing vehicle, you can actually mirror this onto your second vehicle (which is your RV). For that to happen, you obviously need to have existing insurance on another vehicle that you own.
- Reach out to agents or companies who are extremely knowledgeable about RVs. Most people make the mistake of getting an insurance from an entity with limited knowledge of RVs, only to realize they were not covered for their losses because certain things were not clear in the claim.
- Make sure you let the insurance company know that you are going to use your RV as a home, if you are planning that. This allows them to cover the personal belongings you have, as they fall under full-time coverage.
- If you would like, you can even cover roadside assistance, but that may require a little more spending. However, think about this option and compare it to all the roadside assistance companies the insurance companies work with.

RVer Health Insurance

At the end of the day, your health matters, so protect it as much as you can. You can make use of RVer health insurance options provided by many companies. However, use the tips provided in the previous section to find the right insurance for you.

Remember, due diligence is the new prudence. I completely made that up, but you get the point.

After all of the preparations made for your RV, it is time to look into the actual journey. More importantly, getting to know more about camping, boondocking, and other important components of the RV lifestyle.

CHAPTER 5
Camping and Boondocking Basics

If you are new to camping, then the idea of 'boondocking' might sound rather alien to you. However, if you have been researching it, you might have some idea of what it is. Either way, it is best to find out more about the various activities for your RV.

In other words, get ready for the fun stuff.

WHAT IS BOONDOCKING ALL ABOUT?

When you are boondocking, you are camping without any hookups. What do I mean by hookups? Well, the term is used to refer to water, electricity, or sewer facilities. Boondocking means you are planning to go off the grid.

Basically, it is the idea that you get off the highway and stay at free locations without the presence of too many amenities or only use amenities when and if they are available.

The main purpose of boondocking is to disconnect yourself from the electrical or virtual world, make time for yourself, and simply enjoy your surroundings. This is probably one of the most popular reasons for RVing—the idea that you can immerse yourself in nature without thinking about all the things you consider important in your real life (such as phones and internet connection).

Boondocking can also be possible while you are connected as well. Boondockers prefer national parks where they can park for free.

HOW TO CAMP FOR FREE ALL OVER THE WORLD

One of the important things to consider before you begin boondocking is to check for more information about camping sites. Research thoroughly where you are allowed to park for free, and where you might have to pay a certain fee for keeping an RV parked for an extended period. Typically, anything outside city limits is available without restrictions, but that also depends on the local laws.

Here are the rules on camping or boondocking in various places around the world:

North America

Across the continent, there are hundreds of places where you can camp for free. All you need to do is be aware of where these locations are. You could use the apps I provided earlier, or you can make use of www.freecampsites.net to check out places where you can park for free.

Apart from that, you should know that public lands are not always free, but there are often dispersed camping areas close to these public lands. Knowing about these areas is important because they allow you to camp for free. To find out more about these dispersed lands, you can perform your own little online search or use the website www.recreation.gov.

This might come as a surprise to you, but you can also use Walmart parking lots to camp overnight for free. However, make sure you are not sleeping outside or pitching a tent, not only because it is not allowed in some areas, but also for your own safety. Additionally, try not to stay in the parking lot for too long. Some people end up staying for two weeks and ruin the experience for other RVers.

Mexico, Central and South America

Apart from a few sites, you are not going to find a lot of free camping spots in Mexico. For those that are available, you can find them thanks to the charity of the locals, through word-of-mouth information, or because of your own sense of adventure. An important thing to note is that if you are planning to camp somewhere, you have to learn about the local area. Make sure you are safe and are aware of your surroundings. I would recommend www.ontheroadin.com/rv-mexico-2/ if you are looking for camping spots, but most, if not all, will require you to pay.

Central and South America have quite a few options if you are looking for free spots to camp. One of the things you can do is find a hostel and ask if you could use their parking spot. They might allow you to use it for free or for a modest fee. The Central American border crossings can be quite dangerous, so try and plan your trip in advance if you intend to cross borders. In many cases, the locals are quite helpful and may point you in the direction of free campsites. You can always check out national and local parks as they either offer camping there for free or for a truly paltry fee.

Fortunately for many campers, wild camping is quite prevalent in many areas in Central and South America. Wild camping basically means that you find a spot and put down a tent wherever you are. Especially in Central and South America, there are many landscapes that make this type of camping truly worth it. You can usually find free camping (called "camping libre" or "camping agreste" in the local language) or low-cost private campgrounds in cities and the countryside.

iOverlander (www.ioverlander.com) is a great resource to find such areas where you can locate camping grounds to set up your tent. However, the platform does not provide the price of setting up camps, which is usually a really small fee, so you may have to research a location before you head there.

Europe

Much of Europe can be your camping playground, however, there are still restrictions in certain areas.

One thing to note is that Europe has an abundance of backpackers, wild campers, and RVers. You might have a little trouble in Greece since camping for free is actually illegal, but it turns out no one really cares about that and you can often find campers setting up tents and other vehicles in some areas. Do note that you cannot stay for long in these areas as it might draw the attention of the local authorities. While the authorities are not strict, they still might enforce the law if they discover you have been in one location for too long (this makes them suspicious).

But when it comes to other parts of Europe, you can find campgrounds either within the cities or on the outskirts. And, of course, they are free! In fact, many of the camping options in Europe are just as beautiful as the ones in North America. There are many other campgrounds that might require you to pay, but the sights are worth it.

Make sure you are following the rules of the region. Some areas do not allow noise levels to be high beyond a certain time limit. That means no shouting, "I'm king of the world!" after midnight.

Australia and New Zealand

Similar to North America, you can find numerous camping grounds and national parks littered throughout Australia. While you are more likely to run into low-cost camping grounds, that does not mean free camping grounds are not available. You could also make use of truck stops, rest areas, and numerous parking lots. However, you may not be allowed to stay there for long, depending on the area and location. If you are not certain about an area, then make sure you learn more about it before setting up for the night. You could be fined $200 or more for parking in areas not meant for camping. Many RVers have made the mistake of blindly assuming an area allows them to park their motorhomes. WikiCamps has been recommended as one of the best apps to find various camping sites around Australia (including our favorite type: FREE).

New Zealand also offers many options for camping. Check out this website—www.camping_nz.rankers.co.nz/filters/campgrounds—to look for camping sites for your RV throughout the country.

Alternatively, you can use the app Spaceships, which provides camping info and sites in both Australia and New Zealand.

Africa

While free camping is definitely available, it is not common. You might find that most grounds are protected by the local authorities, as they are highly wary of poachers and illegal hunting activities.

But more importantly, the thing you should be concerned about is not whether there is a campground (because camping in Africa is quite common), but rather, the wildlife. You are going to be surrounded by all kinds of animals and creatures. If you are not prepared or are unaware of the local terrain, you might find yourself unable to deal with local wildlife, which includes elephants, baboons, hyenas, lions, tigers, and rhinos. And these are just the creatures you can see. Mosquitos, snakes, and other wildlife are present throughout Africa. However, the country also boasts some of the most incredible sights you may come across. Your best bet is to find a local guide, or someone who is familiar with the place you are camping in, who can talk to the local tribes (whom you might have to pay for using camping grounds) and give you important tips on navigating through the terrain and dealing with the wildlife.

Once again, you can refer to iOverlander to look at numerous camping locations submitted by other users. You should still perform your own research, though, before venturing into any of the camps.

Asia

If I start talking about Asia in detail, I might need an entire book. Or maybe two. But I will try and cover those areas where camping is most prevalent.

China

There are not a lot of campsites and grounds in China. Part of the reason for this is that the culture in the country does not believe in or indulge in the idea of RVing around the country or camping in general. That being said, there are a few camping sites you can make use of for free. For example, tour operators set up camping colonies near the Great Wall.

I would recommend that you do not camp too close to the cities, or you might attract too much attention. Try to blend in and stay in lower lying areas away from roads, lakes, and more traveled areas. You can try to ask locals for help and, in quite a few cases, you may be invited into their homes.

The last piece of advice I can give you is that if you do get caught, then play dumb. You are a foreigner. You didn't know about the rules. You have never come across such information. Who are you again?

Tibet, Mongolia, and Singapore

You are not going to find free camping areas in these countries. In fact, Singapore has no areas where you can camp without paying a fee. Mongolia might be a bit more lenient on camping activities, but you will likely need a guide to show you where you can wild camp. Typically, nobody troubles you, as long as you are not causing them any inconvenience.

Southeast Asia: Thailand, Malaysia, Vietnam, Cambodia, Laos

These countries are similar to Mongolia. Nobody bothers you if you do not bother them. Make sure you are aware of the local laws and the good practices. There are many spots to camp, but you might find that the local insect population could be a pain in the nether region. Research about fauna and what you can do to prevent infections and diseases.

RV CLUBS AND MEMBERSHIPS

When in doubt, join a club. The benefits of being part of a community are many. You get to know about all the campsites and their details. You have a group of people who share the same passion as you. Practically any piece of information one could ever need about RVing is at your fingertips. You can make informed decisions about insurance, locations, journeys, support services, or other various important requirements for your RV life.

There are many clubs you can be a part of. I have narrowed down a few for you to consider.

Passport America

This club is ideal for those who wish to camp for more than just a few nights in a year. You might be able to save a lot of money on camping fees and facilities.

The app has over 1,800 participating campgrounds as part of their network, so you can get discounts at various locations across the country.

One of the great features of the app is that you can actually check prices, discounts, amenities, pictures, and any discount restrictions on all participating campgrounds on the main page itself. This allows you to decide if you would really like to be a member of the club.

Escapees RV Club

What makes Escapees RV Club attractive is the fact that they cater to both newbies and professional RVers. As a member, you can access numerous support groups and discounts. The stand-out feature is that they offer RV classes, which you can take either in person or online. Each of these classes helps you to familiarize yourself with your vehicle, learn to troubleshoot, journey in comfort, and essentially learn all the important tips and tricks of your RV.

They have over 1,000 participating campsites across the country, and discounts range anywhere from 15 to 50%.

Escapees also provides you with Rainbow Parks. These are parks that let you choose from different camping options: short-term, long-term, leases, and deeded lots for sale. Currently, there are seven Rainbow Parks, located in Alabama, Arizona, Florida, Missouri, New Mexico, Tennessee, and Texas. These parks are rather upscale because they offer a lot of amenities along with just parking space. You have access to laundromats, supermarkets, dog parks, and so much more.

Good Sam Club

This is a rather popular club even though they only offer 10 to 30% discounts. The main reason for this is that they have over 2,400 participating campsites. So while they don't provide higher discounts than the other clubs on this list, they do include plenty of options to choose from. For an extra fee, they also provide roadside assistance for your RV, along with other features, such as tire and wheel protection, insurance, and additional services. New RVers would greatly benefit from this club because of the discounts they can get for buying essential products from one of the club's partners, Camping World. This includes protective clothing and gear, propane tanks, supplies, and more.

LONG-TERM AND SHORT-TERM PARKING OPTIONS FOR YOUR RV

Going into long-term RVing means finding spots where you can park your RV, either for a long term, where you are planning on staying in that particular location for a few months, or short-term, where you would like to be there for longer than just a few days, but still intend to leave for another location soon.

What you should look at is not just the duration of your stay, but other features as well. Let me show you what I mean.

Long-Term Stays

Once you have decided that a long-term stay is indeed the option for you, you have to figure out just where you are going to park that giant beast of a vehicle. While you are considering this, you might also want to think about some other important stuff.

Since you are planning to live long-term, are you okay being a part of nature? Or would you prefer to have access to amenities? Would you like to be located in areas that offer certain activities, like hiking or watching a movie at the local cinema? Do you want to be a part of a community?

The reason you have to ask yourself the above questions is because staying somewhere for a longer period of time means you may like to have certain aspects of your normal life as part of your RV lifestyle. So think about the place you would like to live in. For example, do you enjoy surfing and kayaking? Are you the kind of person who enjoys hiking? Additionally, would you like to have certain conveniences nearby, such as a laundromat, gym, or a grocery store? Do you feel more comfortable with a pharmacy close to you? Would you like to participate in local community centers or churches?

All of these questions might help you figure out where you would like to stay. You can choose from the many RV parks available throughout the country—you'll actually find that many RV parks offer long-term discounts. You might not necessarily find them on the websites, however, so your best bet is to actually get in touch with these parks and try to negotiate a deal.

Many of the long-term RV parks will offer monthly rates at a few hundred dollars and will also provide you with additional amenities, like electricity, water, and possibly sewer, cable, and WiFi. Of course, the way these amenities are available may also vary from park to park. For example, some parks offer "free WiFi" that is so crowded, you might as well send carrier pigeons to Google headquarters to get your information faster.

Short-Term Stays

You don't really have to worry too much about short-term stays. There are many options you can make use of, including dedicated apps (that were mentioned earlier) to find nearby short-term RV parks. However, I would also recommend that you get the app, "Oh, Ranger! Park Finder." This is a truly useful tool because it is a complete database of every national and state park in the U.S. This means no matter where you are, you can find the closest RV park to you. One of the other features of the app is that it includes information about each park, as well as activities you can take part in while you're there.

I would also recommend that even if you find such RV parks, it is best if you call them directly and see if you can get any discounts or benefits for your RV stay. Most of these parks don't like to advertise their promotions and offers, so you might have to do a little bit of legwork to get this information.

CHAPTER 6
Making Money on the Road

How much money do you think you will need for your RV on a monthly basis? $4,000? $10,000? $15,000, if you are planning to live in upscale areas and using expensive features?

Regardless of what amount you think you need, there might be one thought that comes to your head—how am I going to get money while I travel?

It is nice to look at travel blogs, BuzzFeed, or other such websites and see how easy it is for many people to find jobs, but it doesn't always work that way. You might also come across blogs where people claim to have saved (insert insane saving amount here) while they were traveling. All you need to do is purchase their quick guide for $49.99.

Let's not kid ourselves. If someone knew the secret formula for success and saving money, they would not be selling it online. Have you ever heard

Elon Musk come on an advertisement and say, "For just $349.99, you get to know all the secrets of getting a machine to the moon! Limited offer only. Terms and conditions apply."

But do not despair, this does not mean you cannot find sources of income while you are on your RV journey. Here are some ways you can look for work to get yourself some cash.

FINDING SEASONAL WORK

One of the best parts about seasonal work is that there is always demand for temporary labor. By keeping pace with the seasons, you can find temporary work as a camping guide, on boats, in bars or restaurants, and many other places.

Here are a few types of seasonal jobs that are usually available:

Retail

You might come across stores with a "help wanted" sign on their front. This is the easiest way to find retail jobs that are seasonal. One of the best ways to do this is to walk around a mall or downtown and stop in to fill out applications. But this also means you'll need to find an RV park close to a mall and other shopping amenities. When you are looking for jobs, make sure you and your employer are clear about your work duration. You wouldn't want them thinking you are going to work there for at least four months when you are planning on leaving after month two.

You can also check out local job portals to get an idea of other temporary work available in the area you are in.

Temps

You can also make use of temp agencies looking for temporary work to fill in for staff who have gone on holiday. Making use of portals, such as Manpower, Snelling & Snelling, and Kelly Services, will allow you to quickly search for temp jobs in the area. Temping is an industry that has always shown growth and for that reason, there is usually no shortage of jobs.

Delivery

Logistical and delivery companies often need more staff during certain seasons. One such example is UPS, who actually have options to hire for seasonal work, as they could always use the extra help. You could also look at the DHL website to find out about seasonal delivery work.

But delivery does not have to be restricted to just parcels and packages. Many restaurants and fast food chains are usually posting job openings for food delivery positions as well. This also goes for certain ecommerce businesses, like Amazon.

Outdoors

When we talk about working outdoors, we are talking about resorts and public areas. These places are always looking for additional help not only for their activity areas, but for the restaurants, bars, and other facilities they offer.

Many of the hospitality, travel, and tourism agencies and companies offer numerous seasonal job opportunities you can take advantage of.

Finding Seasonal Work

Of course, having such jobs available is one thing, but finding them is another. As mentioned earlier, you can take a walk around the local mall to look for job openings.

However, one of the most effective ways to find work is to look into job portals. There are plenty of options for you. Some of the popular ones are Indeed.com, LinkUp.com, SimplyHired.com, and CoolWorks.

com. The reason for their popularity is their advanced search function that allows you to specifically look for seasonal jobs. You can also use keywords and narrow down the location to your area to look for jobs around you. By simply typing, "seasonal," "seasonal holiday," "seasonal retail," "seasonal summer," or any other appropriate keyword brings up numerous listings.

In some cases, you can look at the job listings and, rather than send applications through the website, you can get in touch with the companies directly.

Other websites I can recommend you look into are Seasonworkers.com and SummerJobs.com.

WHY FREELANCE WORK MIGHT BE RIGHT FOR YOU

The best thing about freelance work is that the job satisfaction is entirely up to you. The reason freelancing work is on the rise nowadays is because of the flexible working hours that provide freelancers a healthier work-life balance. This balance is something you might be looking for, especially if you are traveling in an RV.

Still, there are a few things to think about before entering freelance work.

Your Working Hours Are Yours

When you are working as a freelancer, you can choose the hours you put into your work. This will depend on the project you are working on and how many different projects you can handle at one time. You can balance the hours you put in based on your work strategy. For example, you can work constantly for seven days a week and then take a three-day break. The way you work depends entirely on you. You could even put in 12 to 15 hours per day for four days and completely unwind for the remaining three days. The scheduling of your job is entirely up to you.

There is no paid vacation when you are working as a freelancer, but there is such a thing as taking time off and not answering to anyone.

You Are the Accounts Person

When you are freelancing, then you have to be the one to chase after the money owed to you. It's your responsibility to negotiate your working rates, and even if your work delivers incredible value, you may have to be able to justify the cost. Additionally, it is also up to you to reject or confirm extra requests. When you hear phrases such as, "Just take a look at something," or "Give it a quick glance," it usually means, "Can you do this for free?" and "When you start taking a quick glance, I am going to add more tasks to your plate." This means you really need to have a thick skin (metaphorically speaking) to navigate the world of freelance working and pay negotiations.

You Are on Your Own

While you could join a freelancing community and seek assistance from other freelancers, for the most part, you are on your own. You cannot rely on coworkers or team members to help you out during a fix. If there is a challenge that awaits you, then you are the one who will eventually deal with it.

With that being said, are you willing to do freelance work? Here are some places where you can find freelance work:

- Upwork
- Guru
- Freelancer.com
- Mechanical Turk
- Toptal (most of the work here is geared towards finance and software development, but check it out and see if there are opportunities within your field)
- Fiverr

- Freelancermap.com (focuses on IT projects only)
- FlexJobs
- People Per Hour
- OnSite
- iFreelance

It is always better to look at multiple platforms, as that allows you to check out a plethora of jobs in the market before you narrow down your options to just one.

WORKING AT THE CAMPGROUND

Does the idea of finding a job that is dog-friendly, rent-free, and outdoors sound appealing to you? Do you think such a job could not exist? Well, that is exactly what you get when you work in an RV campground.

Campground hosts, or workampers, manage campgrounds across the country. In many occasions, they actually offer free tent and RV space in exchange for the work. You could be doing something rather simple, such as greeting guests, answering questions, doing routine maintenance, light cleaning, and possibly collecting campground fees. In return, you can get to use the campground facilities and spaces free of charge.

Alternatively, if you are looking for a paid job, you can find that as well, but you won't be able to enjoy the other free benefits provided by the campgrounds.

Every campsite is unique and offers its own set of services and work opportunities. For the most part, these are simple jobs you won't have to stress about too much. However, the drawback to that is you won't be earning enough to have extra spending capabilities. If you are indeed looking at the amount of pay you get in return, then make sure you are focused on freelancing work or other kinds of temporary employment.

HOW TO START EARNING PASSIVE INCOME ONLINE

There is one rule when you are thinking of earning passive income, which is there are no get-rich-quick schemes. If you have come across someone who is trying to make you buy some incredible money-earning mechanism, then you have officially come across a snake oil salesman.

But that doesn't mean it isn't possible to earn passive income online. You can, but you still have to put in the effort to make it happen.

Here are some ways you can earn passive income:

Try Out Index Funds

Index funds provide you with a way to invest in the stock market that is completely passive. For example, if you put your money into an index fund based on the S&P 500 Index, you will be investing in the general market. This way, you have to look at how the market functions over a certain period of time, and then you can earn money back on your investment. However, do note that in the world of investments, the lower the risk, the lower the payoff, so you can't expect to spend a certain amount of money and then walk away with a million dollars. Sure, those things happen in movies, but movies never show all the steps that led to the eventual earning of said million dollars.

Make YouTube Videos

These days, almost everyone wants to make videos on YouTube. The sheer number of content creators is just astounding. If you would like to start a YouTube channel for a particular topic, chances are there already exists a channel (or even multiple channels) all about that specific thing. This means you are probably going to be competing with other, more established, content creators on the platform.

But don't let that deter you from starting your own channel.

The main attraction of YouTube lies in the variety of content available for you to work with, ranging from gaming to food to travel. You can create videos for just about any area you would like—music, tutorials, opinions, comedy, movie reviews—and then put them online.

But wait, how does one earn money through YouTube? The setup is fairly simple, you just link Google AdSense to the videos. This will create advertisement overlays and allow promoters to use your channel to show their video ads. There are so many different kinds of ad formats these promoters can use.

The main thing to note is not just any channel can start showing ads on their videos. There are certain criteria you need to meet:

- You need to become part of the YouTube Partner Program
- You need to have accumulated at least 4,000 hours of video watch-time for your videos within the past 12 months
- You need to have at least 1,000 subscribers on your channel

Sure, that does sound like a lot of work, but the payoff is usually good. And besides, you are making videos on things you enjoy.

Affiliate Marketing

You've probably seen this term thrown around a lot these days. You might wonder, is this another scam by people who simply want to target desperate people? Not so. Sure, there are many scams revolving around affiliate marketing, but almost all of them come into the "get this secret technique for X amount of dollars" category.

Affiliate marketing is real, and just about anybody can do it. Here is how it works:

You first have to find a portal that allows you to sign up for affiliate marketing. You then promote certain products or services on your site, for which you will be paid either a flat fee or a percentage of the amount of the resulting sale.

Let's take an example right here. You head over to Amazon (one of the popular platforms for affiliate marketing) and notice a company called AirBrushed (totally made that name up, by the way) selling a new kind of bladeless fans. They are looking for people to promote their products. You sign up on Amazon for affiliate marketing and choose AirBrushed's bladeless fans as the product you would like to market. You then receive a link. You put that link on your website or on your YouTube channel, and that's it. Now, everytime someone clicks on your link and makes a purchase, you get a small percentage of the sale, or a fixed amount in return. Why? Because you were responsible for the sale of said product.

Of course, the whole trick is to market the product so people can click into it, but that is essentially the gist of the entire affiliate marketing program.

And it is completely legal. In fact, as I mentioned earlier, Amazon is a popular option for affiliate marketing.

Photography

Do you enjoy taking pictures? Consider uploading all your photos on websites such as Shutterstock and iStockphoto. That way, if anyone comes across your image and downloads it, you get a small percentage as a commission.

And that's just for one photo. As you begin to upload more and more, you increase the opportunities and channels of cash flow source. This is because your photos can be sold again and again. You simply need to create your photo portfolio, put it on one or more platforms, and then start passively earning money on the photos downloaded.

Write an eBook

The one drawback to this is the fact that it takes a lot of time, initially, to write your ebook. But once you have done so, you can publish it, market it, and begin earning money on its purchase. Of course, the marketing is another aspect that might take a while, but the rewards are plentiful if you succeed.

There are many self-publishing platforms you can take advantage of. Obviously, Amazon is popular for self-publishers. You simply have to send across your book for review and once it has passed the test, it becomes available on the platform. After that, you can get your friends and family to purchase the book and provide a rating on it. Each purchase and rating helps you get your ebook to a better position, thereby increasing your sales even more.

Sell Your Products on the Internet

If you have a special skill, why not sell your creations online? Do you enjoy pottery? Are you a skilled painter? Enjoy making mittens? Whatever you do can be sold online.

In today's world, finding a place where you can reach a wide audience is not difficult. It is the work that goes into marketing your products that is challenging. If you have been on Instagram, then you already know the platform is made for people looking to sell what they create, from fancy art collectibles to cute toys to even clothing and apparel. In fact, you could partner up with a local business, create an online platform for them, and market their products while earning a commission through your work.

If you are good at something, then you can create your own set of instruction or lesson videos and then sell them online. You can use platforms such as Udemy (by far the most popular one) to create courses for people and earn money every time someone buys those courses.

Invest in Real Estate

This is not exactly a way to earn passive income. In fact, you could say that it is semi-passive. However, once you have established the property and maintained it well, it is really only a matter of marketing it properly.

Of course, the downside to all of this is you may need to come up with the initial investment and, based on the property, this could be a small or large amount. But the good thing about real estate is that you can invest in a wide variety of properties based on your budget and requirements. For example, you can invest in apartments, condos, villas, small houses, large houses, and any other type of property you think you are capable of investing in and maintaining.

Additionally, there are professional property managers who can manage your real estate investments for you, usually for around 10% of the monthly rent. These professional managers can help you make your investment more passive (since they will be putting in most of the hard work), but will take a bite out of your returns. My recommendation is to know all the details about the agent before you consider working with them.

Rent Out Your Home

You can even rent out your home to people who would like to live there temporarily. You can list your property on short-term rental platforms, such as Airbnb. People will use your property for as long as they have booked it online and then move on.

You will need to have someone around to help maintain the house while you are gone, but you can easily do this by enlisting the help of someone you know and paying them for their efforts.

Of course, the drawback to this is that you are going to be allowing complete strangers into your home. You might not know about their character or behavior. However, most platforms (such as Airbnb) allow you to first get in touch with the guests and talk to them before you agree to anything. This way, you can be comforted by knowing that the person staying in your home is not someone who might destroy anything.

Silent Partnership

Do you know of a business that is in need of some capital? If that is indeed the case, then you can become an angel investor in that business. But rather than offering your capital in the form of a loan, you can purchase an equity position in the business. This means you earn revenue based on the profit-sharing rules put into place. The business owner will, of course, take care of the business, but you will be earning eventual profits because of your investment.

Jeremy Frost

CHAPTER 7
Solo RVing Done Right

THERE IS SOMETHING magnificent about solo adventuring. In fact, you might have seen the recent trend where people prefer to travel the world on their own. They save up for a long time, plan out their journey, pack their bags, and off they go. They enjoy every aspect, like finding an exotic location, experiencing the local food, being a part of many adventures, and simply discovering more things by themselves.

Solo adventure is 'the thing' these days.

The same applies for solo RVing. It is similar to traveling alone as a backpacker. The only difference is that you are traveling on board a moving home with a lot of comforts thrown in.

DON'T LET BEING BY YOURSELF STOP YOU!

Solo traveling is not a lonely experience. Many people might say otherwise, but there is something liberating about experiencing the world on your own.

However, taking on the journey all by yourself can be a pretty intimidating task. After all, you have to figure out a lot of the stuff by yourself, but this does not have to be the case (hint: you have this book).

First, we are going to dispel a few fears of solo RVing.

It's Not Safe

Solo RVing presents the same types of risks that group traveling does. However, there are a few advantages of solo RVing—there are less chances for human errors, you are not easily distracted, there is less need to make frequent pit stops, and other such scenarios that could develop when you are traveling with others.

But what about the dangers from external sources? I generally think the worries about solo RVing are typically blown out of proportion. People complain about how you could be robbed while on the road. This is not just restricted to solo RVers. People who travel in groups have as much danger of being robbed as people who travel alone. In fact, if you are with someone else, things can even get a bit more complicated because you are now concerned for both yourself and the other person. The news loves to talk about break-ins and thefts by putting the focus on solo traveling, but they fail to cover stories about families and groups who have faced the same problems.

At the same time, you still need to be prepared to face some of these dangers while you are traveling alone. After all, the drawback to it is that you are usually left to fend for yourself, without any assistance. We shall look at some safety techniques you can adopt while you are on the road later in this chapter.

It Can Be Overwhelming

You are going to be in charge of every aspect of taking care of and driving your RV. Checking for maintenance? You are going to be doing that. Washing the tanks? You are responsible for that, and you cannot ask anyone to take over. Meal preparing? Once again, you.

At this point, I might not be painting a nice picture for you to think about when traveling alone. In fact, I might have convinced you to call up any of your old friends whom you haven't kept in touch for years just to accompany you on your journey. You might be willing to pay them, as well.

But that won't be necessary. You see, one of the things about solo RVing are the rewards you can gain from it. You become more independent. You gain confidence since you have to deal with everything. There is also the fact that while things are overwhelming in the beginning, you don't have to handle all of them at the same time.

It's like asking a chef to prepare the starter, main course, dessert, and drinks simultaneously, while also cleaning up the kitchen space and checking for supplies. But what if the same chef was allowed to deal with each task independently?

In a similar manner, you don't have to deal with everything in one go. Take your time to go through the tasks. There is no hurry. After all, you are going to be spending a long time on the road, so take it easy. Let the learning process itself become an adventure.

Loneliness

A lot of people are under the impression that getting into an RV and soloing it around the world can get a bit lonely. However, what separates solo RVing from being part of a crowd is that you can actually interact with people as you see fit. You are free to meet anyone you would like on your journey. Besides, RVing is not exactly a lonely activity. There are tons of social platforms and groups that allow anyone to meet interesting people on their journeys.

You can actually become part of a community by looking for them online. Each stop you make is filled with the pleasure of encountering unique people and making new friends.

Difficult

People sometimes think getting started with solo RVing is more difficult compared to getting started with a group. This is probably because of the idea that only one person will be taking care of the downsizing and preparations. Although this might be true, they forget to think about one important factor—the more people there are in an RV, the more packing you may need to do and the more space-conscious you have to be.

If you are traveling solo, then you are going to have enough space to carry a lot of equipment. Additionally, by traveling solo, you only need to think about what items you need for yourself, eliminating lengthy downsizing processes.

That means no more thinking about whether you need to make more room for your shoes or someone else's. It's your ride. It's your rules.

You are the master of your trip. You are the commander of your vehicle. You are—

Well, you get the point.

STAYING SAFE ON THE ROAD

First things first—stay on the beaten track. Try to follow what others have been doing for years, and don't take unnecessary risks.

Apart from that, here are tips you can take while you are on the road:

- When you are tucking in for the night, make sure you have locked your doors and are aware of where you are parked. If you notice too many beer bottles scattered around in your area, it probably is not a sign of a peaceful place with wonderful people around.
- If you have RV neighbors, let them know you are traveling alone. They will be able to watch out for you.
- Keep your friends and family informed about your route. Let them know where you are,

and get some advice if they know about the location you are staying in.
- If you notice that your RV is the only one in the vicinity, there is probably a good reason why. Try to find company.
- If you are staying overnight in a parking lot, stay under a light and, preferably, in front of a security camera. Bonus points for parking next to the security booth.
- Check and see if you are getting good phone reception in the area where you plan to stay. Remember, most horror movie plots take a turn for the worse when the characters know they have lost their phone signals.
- If you feel like something feels "off" about the place you are about to stay in, then trust your instincts.
- When you leave your RV, but are unsure of the neighborhood, close your blinds, lock the vehicle securely, and keep all your valuables inside.
- Keep air horns, alarms, or any other preventive measures in your RV just in case your shouting voice is not too loud.
- There are so many places where you can camp for free, but still remain with a group of RVers.

- If you are taking extra precautions when you are staying with your RV, such as adding locks to all the storage spaces inside your vehicle, that is a smart move. Do not let anyone convince you that what you are doing is extreme.
- If something is too good to be true, then it usually is.

AVOIDING LONELINESS

Solo travel is fun, there is no denying that. But many people often ponder upon the loneliness that RV traveling can bring.

Now, before we talk about dealing with loneliness, it is important to understand the distinction between being lonely and being alone. On one hand, you have the feeling of being alone. When you are alone, you have either chosen to be in that state or it has happened to you involuntarily. Either way, you are not comfortable with the situation. On the other hand, you have the feeling of loneliness—where you are aware that you are on your own and it has an effect on your emotional and mental state, typically a negative response. One is a state of being, while the other is an emotional response.

Additionally, one has to take into account that certain people are introverted while others are extroverted, which means some people don't mind spending time with themselves while others are social butterflies. In other words, some people rarely go out to meet people and are comfortable boondocking in the woods, away from civilization, while others need to be as close as possible or within the limits of a community, town, city, or other such areas.

So, how are the differences between loneliness and lonesomeness connected to being an introvert or extrovert, especially when it comes to RVing? Simple enough. Introverts can spend time by themselves without being affected by feelings of loneliness. Extroverts might feel lonely when they do not engage with other people for a long time. This is something you have to think about with regards to your RV adventure. Would you like to explore the wilderness and the sights on your own (or with your dog or other pets as company)? Or do you prefer to stop somewhere and get to know the locals?

Once you have decided on your preferred way to enjoy your RV life, then think about how you can keep in touch regardless of where you are. Here are some tips you can follow:

Connection #1: Your Family and Friends

Make sure you do not lose touch with those close to you, whether they are your family, distant cousins, friends, or even Casper the Friendly Ghost (if you happen to know such an entity). When you are connected to people close to you, you are always aware of their presence. You know they are thinking about you, excited to know about your adventures, and are concerned when something happens to you. Additionally, there is a strong bond that keeps you from feeling lonely no matter where you are.

Besides, home is where the heart is. Your RV is your home, but your family and friends are a part of that home even if they are not physically present there.

Connection #2: Join Communities

There are so many RV communities out there to be a part of. Not only can you meet interesting people, but if you happen to make friends in the community, you can find out where their friends are located and drive over to the campground or area they are located in.

Alternatively, you can find out which RV park has a large number of people so you can head over there.

There are communities that can help you find out if there are any RV-related events in your area, as well as guide you towards where you want to go next from your current location. Not only that, but they can also inform you of other RVers who have set up their motorhomes in a specific location for a long term, including just how long they have been there.

Communities are not only a great place to meet people, but can also provide some valuable information (as we touched on earlier).

Connection #3: Meet People You Know All Over the Country

There is no rule that says once you are in your RV, all you have to think about is nature, isolation, and cleaning out your black tank once in a while. You are free to go wherever you would like, so try and visit some friends living in other parts of the country. Not only will you experience a wonderful journey along the way, but you may just have a wonderful reunion.

Connection #4: FOMO

Sometimes, when you feel lonely, it might not be because of the lack of people around you. Perhaps it is due to the situation you find yourself in. You might have what people like to refer to as "FOMO," or the "Fear of Missing Out." You could be thinking about:

How your current situation can be much better than it is

The state of your situation as compared to others

You might be wondering if things would be different if you had started a business or if you had simply completed that PhD in university. Perhaps you should have listened to your parents, your boss, your friends, or that voice in your head. All of these thoughts start nagging at you because, for the first time, you actually feel liberated. Our minds are rather funny things. When we are having fun, it automatically starts to think of some rather negative thoughts. It's as though your mind loves to keep you disappointed. But that is the mind's defense mechanism going into action. It is trying to prevent you from receiving any unpleasant surprises in the future, and so it runs through all the potential scenarios. However, what you must do is be in the present. Don't worry about the "what ifs." Live in the moment.

Don't worry about what other people have. Comparison is the thief of joy. When we compare, we are never going to be content. Eventually, we are going to start feeling different from other people. That, in turn, makes us feel lonely.

Connection #5: Being Absent from the Present

Sometimes, it might not be easy to be in the present. There is a real challenge to living this way because, most often, we are thinking about various situations, people, ideas, and goals.

Try to learn how to keep your mind focused on the present, or what most people would say, in the act of 'mindfulness.' Keep your thoughts from straying away too far from the present day. It is going to be a challenge, but as you get involved in the day-to-day activities of your RV, you will find that it gets much easier. Don't worry too much about the things you have no control over. As you begin to take care of your RV, yourself, the job you have while in the RV, and the community you become a part of, all of the things that make you feel lonely will start dwindling away.

Connection #6: Boredom

Sometimes, you might actually not be lonely, but just bored. If you are unaware of what makes you happy or brings joy to you, then you are often going to feel bored on the road. The trouble with boredom is that one does not easily identify it because thinking that we are bored automatically means our lives are not interesting. And that is a thought most people don't like to have.

There is a simple rule when it comes to boredom, which is to accept that you are feeling bored. This immediately makes things easier because if you can identify the fact that you don't have anything to bring joy or energy into your life at the moment, then you can plan to go get it. You could take a walk outside, read your favorite book, take your dog out for a walk, or get in touch with the RV community to ask them where to find some incredible events or activities. Boredom can easily be treated with simple solutions. Loneliness, on the other hand, is a more complex situation and might require evaluation.

CONNECTING WITH THE COMMUNITY

Finding an RV community is not going to be as challenging as one might think. The world of RV traveling is growing, and you can see evidence of this in the number of campgrounds that have appeared within the past few years. Just by looking at the various special facilities for RVs (there's even an RV resort!), you know there is a tremendous interest in motorhomes. And where there is a huge presence of interest, there might just be a community for that interest.

The world of RVing has no deficiency in the number of communities it offers. You can easily find communities online through a quick search or by using some of the ways provided below to become a part of them.

At the Campground or RV Park

Many campgrounds provide you with the opportunity to meet new people. Not only is the campground itself one big community, but chances are many people staying there are a part of a unique community of their own. This provides you with the chance to make friends, find travel companions, and even get some help, should you need it.

In fact, if you have a problem, chances are that one, or many of the people in the community, has gone through it (especially the experienced RVers) so it would benefit you greatly to become a part of a community.

One of the best ways to meet people is to take a walk around the camp. Find people who are sitting together on camp chairs and join them (you will be surprised at how welcoming they can all be). Strike up conversations with your RV neighbors. Feel free to talk to people. Through your connections, you will be able to either form your own community or become part of another.

Exploring

Whether you are fishing, hiking, or exploring the sights of a tourist attraction, you might just bump into fellow RVers. Take a moment to get to know them. You will be surprised at how simple it can be to connect with others. Of course, you may occasionally get the traveler who prefers to avoid social contact, but do not let that deter you from finding meaningful and incredible connections elsewhere.

During your explorations, you are bound to discover local RV communities in or near the town or city you are staying in.

Online

As I mentioned earlier, you can always find communities online. You can perform your own search, but here are some websites you should check out:

- irv2
- Technomadia
- Wheelingit

We have now covered various aspects of the RV world. However, there are still concerns when it comes to RVing. Let's see if we can deal with those situations.

CHAPTER 8
Commonly Asked Questions

IT'S TIME TO "keep it real." Even if RVing is incredible 99% of the time, it is always better to look at the good, the bad, and the ugly of the RV world before heading out on the road.

WHAT IS THE WORST THING ABOUT LIVING IN AN RV?

- Being connected constantly helps you in many ways, but the challenge is to *remain* connected constantly. You might end up in areas where there is no internet connection or mobile service. That results in you trying to find a local café or WiFi hotspot, or worse, looking for the closest area with a connection.
- Be prepared for bad weather. When we are within our homes, the walls are thick so we don't worry about heavy rains or

thunderstorms. When you are in an RV, however, the walls are thinner and the weather has a bigger impact.
- The RV maintenance. Sure, there are steps you can follow to make it easier, but it is still work and no one really likes to do that (except maintenance folks, and even they might scowl at the occasional RV-related upkeep work).
- Some RVs have washers and dryers while others, unfortunately, do not. If your RV is not outfitted with the aforementioned machines, you may be surprised to see just how often you find yourself looking for a laundromat.
- Being lonely. We have offered some advice for dealing with that, though, so make sure you use all the tips you can.

WHAT IS THE BEST THING ABOUT RV LIFE?

- You can live by the beach, mountains, desert, lake, or anywhere else you would like. Want to park somewhere close to the Amityville Horror mansion? You can (though in all honesty, why would you?). The freedom to travel to so many places, experiencing so many things, while living on the road is

a unique feeling that cannot be described unless you have actually lived it.
- When you are living in an RV, you tend to spend more time outside. You are also motivated to enjoy a healthier life. Many RVers have picked up outdoor hobbies such as hiking, jogging, and rafting. You may find yourself beginning to change your life for the better.
- You cannot beat the views you see when you are traveling in an RV.
- You don't need to buy too many things when you are in an RV. You are not held down by materialistic objects; your main focus is the experience and the joy it brings. Every moment in your life is one filled with what you encounter on your journey. If the journey is as important as the destination, then being attached to your belongings is no way to experience that. However, in an RV, you are not distracted by such possessions. You are free to truly live the journey.
- Don't like your neighbors? Move.
- Don't like your surroundings? Move.
- Simply want to move? Move.

- Ever wanted to work and travel? Well, now is your chance.
- If you would like, you can stay in one place for a long time, get to know the people around you, take part in the community, and live among the locals.
- You learn to be independent, develop important life skills, and even build confidence. The RV life can influence you in many positive ways, maybe even making you become a better person.

HOW CAN YOU DO LAUNDRY?

- You can find campgrounds or parks where there are laundromats. By using the apps I recommended earlier, you can seek more information about various sites to find if they have laundry facilities.
- Make use of the local towns or nearby cities, if you can access them.
- In many cases, people learn to do their own laundry by hand. There are many occasions where you'll have to stay somewhere overnight, which means you can wash your clothes and leave them out to dry. However, make sure you are in a safe area before doing

so in case you wake up the next morning and find your favorite polo shirt missing.
- Some RVs come with washers and dryers. You can also add them to your RV, but be very mindful of the space.

DO YOU FEEL SAFE ON THE ROAD?

- Typically, RVing is safe if you follow the rules and use a bit of common sense.
- Do not open the door in the middle of the night to people you do not recognize.
- Don't park your rig in neighborhoods littered with beer bottles and tagged with gang graffiti. That graffiti is not someone's idea of abstract expression—they are warnings.
- Don't keep your RV unlocked while you are outside. Don't keep your RV unlocked while you are inside, as well.
- Your RV probably comes with a bathroom. If you are in an unknown area, avoid public bathrooms.
- Stick to campgrounds and parks meant for RVs.
- I know it sounds nice to put up a sign outside saying, "Our home on wheels—Andy and his golden retriever, Fifi," but you are literally

letting everyone know who is inside the RV. So the next time someone knocks on your door and calls your name, it may not be because they know you, but because they saw your cute sign with puppy stickers.
- Do not leave documents lying about. Keep them out of sight in a safe place.
- Crime on the road? It happens whether you are in an RV or not. If you were driving a vehicle and you felt something wrong while going down a particular path, you would immediately choose another way. Use the same sense when you are in an RV.
- I've mentioned this before, and it is worth mentioning again, keep your friends and family updated about you.

ISN'T GAS MILEAGE TERRIBLE?

- This depends on how you drive your RV. I recommended earlier that you should drive your RV slowly. This is not only for safety, but for gas consumption as well.
- Another important thing to note is that you should turn off the electronics or appliances not in use. There are RVers who leave their television on throughout their ride and

then wonder where all the gas went the next morning. Make sure you are switching off the lights, appliances, or anything else using your RV's power.

WHEN WILL YOU START LIVING A NORMAL LIFE AGAIN?

There is no specific time period for you to get adjusted to the RV life. What is important is to focus on getting used to your new home and establish a routine for the various chores and activities you might take on while traveling on the road.

Additionally, make sure you enjoy the experience. Don't think of the whole process as one big chore or requirement. Appreciate the journey and everything else that comes with it.

CAN YOU RV FULL-TIME IN THE WINTER?

You can. Make sure you are aware of the local weather conditions so you prepare yourself for anything by getting the right gear.

Your RV itself can keep you warm from the elements, but the one thing you might have to be concerned about is the pile-up of snow outside.

Make sure you have a shovel if you are traveling to places where the snow can accumulate.

HOW DO YOU STAY IN SHAPE WHILE ON THE ROAD?

The best part about being in an RV is the opportunity it brings to step outside and indulge in some outdoor activities, so don't hesitate to take a walk or go out hiking whenever you feel like it.

DO YOU GET TIRED OF LIVING IN A SMALL SPACE?

Some people do experience a sense of tiredness when it comes to living in an RV, but they more than make up for it by getting outdoors, being part of communities, or taking part in various activities. Just because you are in an RV does not mean you cannot head out and do something fun!

WHAT DO YOU DO WITH ALL THE POOP?

As mentioned before, you dump everything into special sewer holes or dump stations. I have even provided you tips on how to keep the black tank (or the poop tank) clean.

CONCLUSION

RVing is an adventure. It is about the journey and the way it changes your life. But getting started on this journey can be challenging, which is why you have this book.

We have discussed how you can get started with your RV adventure. We've talked about how you can downsize your home and then pack all the essential items into your RV. We've focused on the different types of RVs you can find and what you should look for when purchasing one. Then, we looked at how you can transition to your RV life, as well as how you can travel with your kids or pets. We have gone through the waste management process and how you can perform maintenance on your RV. We looked at camping and boondocking and even found ways for you to make money while you are on the road. Solo RV was also given a special focus in the book.

With all of this information, you can get started on your RV journey with confidence. Remember to take your time with a particular step if you are feeling unsure or lost. For example, if the downsizing process is turning out to be quite a challenge, then make sure you are not stressing about it or in a hurry. Take your time and do it right. This way, you'll find yourself facing less stress in the future. Additionally, get to know your RV. Familiarize yourself with all its features and mechanisms. Take it out for a test run before you head out on your RV adventure; be comfortable with your rig and the space within. Take your time to learn about the various RV communities, which will allow you to plan your journey better. You know how to store things, what you should do if are in need of assistance, what campgrounds you should go to, and more.

But most importantly, remember to enjoy your journey.

Happy RVing.

REFERENCES

Power, R. (2018). Consumers are Rejecting Materialism and Embracing Experiences — Here's How to Capitalize. Retrieved 14 September 2019, from https://www.inc.com/rhett-power/consumers-are-rejecting-materialism-embracing-experiences-heres-how-to-capitalize.html

RV Passive Income Guide, https://www.amazon.com/dp/B07XFT3NP5/

Made in the USA
Middletown, DE
26 November 2022